THE WORLD
WITHOUT GOD

THE WORLD WITHOUT GOD

MADHAV DESAI

PARTRIDGE

A Penguin Random House Company

To order additional copies of this book, contact
Partridge India
000 800 10062 62
orders.india@partridgepublishing.com

www.partridgepublishing.com/india

CONTENTS

1   Creation of God...11

2   The Administrator God...15

3   The Creator God 23

4   From Darwin to DNA............................. 37

5   Body and Soul 57

6   Fate.. 75

7   Need for Religion...................................... 90

8   Beyond God 99

To Bhai and Ben

For your inspiration, encouragement
And the precious gift

I don't believe in astrology;
I'm a Sagittarius and we're skeptical.

-Arthur C Clarke

Thank God I'm an atheist

- Luis Bunuel

1

CREATION OF GOD

If God did not exist, it would be
necessary to invent Him

- Voltaire

This book opens with two questions:

Does God exist? Did He create this universe and
everything in it, including Man?

My answer to the second question is: No. In fact, *it is
Man who created God.* Initially, out of ignorance, he found
it necessary to imagine the existence of a Supreme Being
to explain all the natural phenomena; and later he started
to believe that the same Supreme Being also controlled the
destiny of each living entity in this universe. Science has
now discovered evidence to suggest that the universe and
the life in it came into existence without a Creator, and
have been running without the help of any external force
or entity.

The answer to the first question? Yes, of course. God
exists. After all, Man has created Him.

Science has made great progress in the past 500 years,
and this progress has accelerated in the last century. We

now have scientific evidence that proves or disproves much of what we had so far accepted as eternal truth. More than anything else, science has given us a rational point of view that questions everything that we had earlier been told to believe; and when you start questioning the very foundations of your belief system, your entire perspective of life and the universe begins to change.

In this book, I have tried to describe my view of this universe, and more specifically, of human life, without depending on concepts which we have been relying on to explain what is happening around us, and what is happening to us. These concepts include the existence of God, the divine mission that we are carrying with us when we landed on this planet, fate or destiny, the concept of soul with existence independent of the body, *atma*, *paramatma*, rebirth, or any form of life after death, divine justice and the role played by *karma* in justifying why certain things happen to some of us and not to the others. These concepts have become so ingrained in our beliefs, that it may offend our sensibility to suspend these beliefs even for a short period. These beliefs don't need proof, we say; we know them to be true because we can feel them. I promise to revisit some of these concepts after I have put forth my thesis, and see how these concepts can be viewed in new light.

It is not difficult to imagine that the early Man was overawed by what he saw around him. The sun rose everyday, in the same direction, traversed across the sky and set in the opposite direction, only to rise again, without fail, after some time. He saw climatic changes: cold, heat and rains, taking place cyclically. He saw rivers flowing: sometimes drying up, sometimes overflowing. He saw tides come and go in the sea. Through experience, he was aware of the limits of his own powers and those of the men and animals who co-existed on Earth; and very clearly, none had the ability to control even the mundane events of his daily life. Who, then, caused all this to happen? Who controlled it? Who ordered gales and tornadoes that caused destruction beyond the powers of any man or animal he had come across? Who caused earthquakes and volcanic eruptions? To the early man, it was very clear that an invisible super power was responsible for the day-to-day, normal happenings, who sometimes decided to unleash his infinite powers to cause havoc in the small world that man was familiar with. This super power was given a name: God.

The concept of God has survived, indeed strengthened, since the early ages. If we analyze our idea of God, and look at things that we have placed under His domain, as they are clearly outside ours, we find Him in four different roles. One is as an *Administrator of the universe*, ensuring that all functions that I have mentioned above, and many more, are carried out — some with meticulous regularity, and some at His whims. The second role is the role of *Creator of the Universe*. After all, somebody must have been responsible to create all that we see around us — galaxies, solar systems and planets. The third role is as *Creator of life* on Earth — from single-celled organisms to the intelligent human life.

But it is in His fourth role that we interact with Him most. This is the role of a *Personal God*, who is intimately involved in our affairs. He answers our prayers, keeps track of our good and bad deeds, and knows when we do them (or even *think* of doing them), forgives or punishes sins, and intervenes in the world by performing miracles.

In the next three chapters, we will discuss the first three responsibilities assigned to God. The rest of the book is devoted to His role as Personal God

———◈———

2

THE ADMINISTRATOR GOD

*If there is something in me which can be
called religious then it is the unbounded
admiration for the structure of the world
so far as our science can reveal it.*

- Albert Einstein

Man's belief in the existence and powers of God started with Him in the role of the Administrator. This was inevitable for reasons we saw in the previous chapter, and is evident from the forms of Gods conceptualized by the early man.

Over the ages of darkness, before man knew more about the world and the forces of nature that acted upon it, he attributed all these forces to God, and tried to appease Him. Man created many versions of God, depending on the specific force that he wished to worship. Thus, Sun was considered a form of God since it gave light and heat, both essential for the survival of man. Water was known to be the lifeline of all living beings, and was an object of worship in all forms. Prayers were offered to Rain Gods with the plea to arrive on time, and to bring just the right quantity of water. River was also seen as God (or Goddess), and the worshippers prayed for a continuous flow, but without fury. Sea Gods were worshipped by seafarers and fishermen, whose livelihood and personal safety depended on these Gods not punishing them by being overly rough.

Different cultures believed in Gods associated with specific powers: there were Gods of Wind, Fire, Thunder, Wealth, Knowledge, Love, Fertility, War, Healing and Death, to cite a few examples. It is evident that all areas where man feared uncertainty and a possibility that an unfavorable turn of events could cause a setback to his hopes, aspirations and smooth functioning of life were imagined to be under control of a super power, whose favors could be gained 'by gifts and entreaties, by prayers and sacrifices to control future events'.[1]

Almost all cultures have personified God. David Hume, the 18th century philosopher, posits a natural propensity in humans to 'conceive all beings like themselves, and to transfer to every object, those qualities, with which they are familiarly acquainted, and of which they are intimately conscious'. Anthropomorphism is the act of depicting gods and goddesses in human forms and possessing human characteristics such as love, and also jealousy and hatred. The Greek gods such as Zeus and Apollo were often depicted in anthropomorphic forms. Some of the avatars of the Hindu god Vishnu possessed human forms and qualities. Creating God in a form and with traits familiar to man made it easy for an average person to picture and think about God. Even the language that God spoke was the same as the language that people in that culture used. This is an indication that

---

[1]   The Natural History of Religion, David Hume (1757)

God existed only in his imagination, which was limited to his everyday experiences.[2]

Even before the advent of science, man had started to unravel the mysteries of nature. Years and years of observation of the time of sunrise and sunset showed a pattern: for example, the duration of the daylight increases and then decreases as we go from one solstice to another. Or that a year follows a climatic cycle. The record of timing and height of tides allowed man to deduce that there were two high tides every day; tides occurred about 45 minutes later each day, and the height of the tide was related to the lunar phase: full moon and new moon days and nights had the highest tides. In fact, with the understanding of nature, it was possible to predict the time of sunrise or the high tide on any day in the future. Or predict the path of the moon and other planets. Exactly why the sun should rise, tides should occur, seasons should change or planets should move in the sky in an orderly fashion was not understood,

---

[2]   Many cultures also imagined their deities to resemble animals, or be half-human and half-animal. Medusa (woman with snakes for hair), Minotaur (half man and half bull) and Pegasus (winged horse) from the Greek mythology; Hanuman (monkey) and Ganesha (Human with an elephant head) from Hindu mythology; Bast (feline head on a woman, daughter of the Sun god Ra) of Egypt and Kukulkan (serpent) in Aztec culture are some examples of Animism. Anthropologists believe that in some cultures, human beings were often regarded on a roughly equal footing with animals, plants, and natural forces. Therefore, it was morally imperative to treat these agents with respect. In this world view, humans were considered a part of nature, rather than superior to, or separate from it. In such societies, ritual was considered essential for survival, as it was believed to win the favor of the spirits of one's source of food, shelter, and fertility and ward off malevolent spirits.

and this was greatly attributed to God, but the predictability showed that God followed certain rules while administering the universe.

Scientific discoveries led by Copernicus, Galileo, Kepler and Newton gave a new perspective of the behavior of nature. Earth, they said was not flat but was round. It was spinning about an axis that was tilted, and was rotating around the sun along an orbit that was elliptical. It explained *why* the sun seemed to move from East to West and *why* climate changed over a year. Newton's laws of gravitation and motion, and Laplace's mathematical interpretation of these laws enabled scientists to compute the motion of Earth, moon and all planets around the sun. If the early astronomers were able to predict the way nature would behave, science not only validated these predictions, but more importantly, explained *why* nature behaved the way it did. There are certain gaps in our scientific knowledge: for example, even today, we are unable to *predict* earthquakes. But this is only a gap that will be filled with more scientific research in seismology. The important thing is that we know exactly what causes earthquakes and tsunamis, and that there are no unknown forces that cause them.[3]

These discoveries were difficult for people to understand and accept – because they challenged the deep-rooted conviction that God administered the universe. On the other hand, the scientific discoveries cited above stand even today, with some modifications, many additions, and some known gaps. The fact that electro-mechanical devices

---

[3]   If Sri Lankan victims of the 2004 tsunami want to know why *they* were made to suffer this catastrophe, it is a legitimate question. But we will deal with such questions later when we discuss *Personal God*.

work is a proof of the validity of these scientific laws. TV, other electronic devices and the atom bomb validate laws of subatomic physics. Science has also discovered the causes (and treatments) of our illnesses and epidemics (they are *not* God's way of meting out punishment); how plants generate food for themselves and why gun powder explodes when we set a match to it. Science has eliminated the need for God as an administrator of the universe, and understandably, therefore, there is considerable debate between scientific thinkers and spiritual thinkers.

Science is the quest for the understanding of how physical reality works. In an effort to unravel the laws that apply to the physical reality, scientists construct models of reality, and a set of rules that relate various physical quantities in the models to one another. These relations are expressed mathematically in the form of mathematical equations. $PV = RT$ is an example of the mathematical representation of a thermodynamic model, that seeks to find a relationship between the pressure exerted on a body of gas (P), the volume of gas (V) and the temperature (T); R being a constant.

Models must make definite predictions about future observations. In $PV = RT$, if the volume of gas and its temperature are measured, the model should be able to predict the gas pressure, which should tally with the observed pressure. Using controlled methods, scientists collect data in the form of records of observable physical evidence of natural phenomena and validate the model.

Models are not reality. They are mere abstractions of certain aspects of reality. They embody a theory or a hypothesis about the behavior of the real nature. A hypothesis, by definition, cannot be proven. It is assumed to be correct, unless proven wrong. No matter how many times the outcome predicted by the model agrees with the observation, the hypothesis cannot be said to be 'proven', because you can never be sure that the next time the result will not contradict it. On the other hand, you can disprove the hypothesis by finding even one observation that disagrees with it[4]. Every time the prediction matches our observation, our confidence in the hypothesis increases; but whenever a new observation disagrees with the prediction, we have to either discard the hypothesis or modify it.

Newton's theory of gravity had stood the test of time for many centuries, before astronomers detected a slight difference in the motion of the planet Mercury, predicted by Newton's theory and actually observed. Einstein's General Theory of Relativity predicted the planet's motion more accurately. After this, General Relativity was considered a more accurate theory than Newton's Gravity Theory to represent celestial movements. For terrestrial motion, the difference in the predictions between the two is so negligible, that Newton's theory is preferred, as it is better understood and is easier to use.

If the objective of science is to discover the laws of nature, it makes two important assumptions. The first is,

---

[4]   There is a degree of confidence attached to a hypothesis. A hypothesis such as: 'It is generally hot before it rains' does not collapse with a single dissenting observation; but the degree of confidence that the reverse (null) hypothesis is correct increases with every such observation. For a hypothesis of statistical nature, 99.5% confidence level may be considered good enough. When you want to assert a scientific law, the degree of confidence of disproving the reverse hypothesis must be 100 %.

that there *are* laws to be discovered. Who has told us that nature *will* obey any laws? So our first hypothesis is that nature works according to laws (not all of them known to us yet). Our observations for millennia have given us sufficient confidence in this hypothesis. Everyday since the beginning of human consciousness, sun has always risen in the East. But if only once, we see the sunrise in the West, all our faith in science and the laws that we have discovered would be lost.

And the second assumption that is crucial in the scientific quest is: *There is no God*. Because if God exists and is free to intervene in the universe and break the laws, we will never be sure of our predictions and hence of the laws that science has discovered. Science abhors miracles, which by definition involve divine intervention. Every time a major miracle has been reported, scientists have analyzed the incident and tried to explain the phenomenon scientifically: whether it was the milk-drinking Ganesha idol in India in 1995 or the miracle in Fatima in Portugal, in 1917, where 'suddenly, impelled by some mysterious force, the sun began to whirl in the sky, casting off great shafts of multicolored light. Red, green, blue, yellow, violet'.[5] Both these are examples where mass hysteria was created over the 'miracle'; but the scientists, after their investigation have not found it necessary to change their theories.

Not all 'miracles' reported till date have been resolved through a scientific explanation. But this is on account of the gap in our understanding of the reality. With the progress of Science and Technology, as the gap is filled, these miracles

---

[5]   http://www.sofc.org/Spirituality/s-of-fatima.htm

will also find an explanation that is properly understood. If a man, who has been asleep for three decades, wakes up today, something as widespread as mobile technology would also seem like a miracle to him. To paraphrase Arthur C Clark, the outcome of any advanced technology, which is not fully understood, is indistinguishable from miracle.

David Hume has suggested this test for a miracle: 'No testimony is sufficient to establish a miracle, unless the testimony be of such a kind, that its falsehood would be more miraculous than the fact which it endeavors to establish.'

3

THE CREATOR GOD

Because there is a law such as gravity, the universe can and will create itself from nothing.

- Stephen Hawking

Although almost all scientists and those who understand and believe in science are now of the view that God has no role to play in the day to day administration of the universe, many of these people see no alternative to the belief that the creation of the universe is not possible without an external force. God may not have a role to play in keeping the sun, moon and the stars in their proper places, because their motion is governed by certain laws, discovered by science; but who made these laws? How did the universe originate? Surely, a force must have acted from outside the universe to originate it.

Atheists counter this argument by asking: If the universe must have a creator, who created the Creator? If a self-created Creator is acceptable, why not a self-created universe? Richard Dawkins, in his *The God Delusion* argues against the possibility of God as a creator thus:

'Any creative intelligence, of sufficient complexity to design anything, comes into existence only as the end product of an extended process of gradual evolution. Creative intelligences, being evolved, necessarily arrive late in the universe, and therefore cannot be responsible for designing it.'

Theists, who are guided by reason, and not blind faith, advance three compelling arguments in favor of external super intelligence having played a role in the creation of the universe:

No Free Lunch

There must have been a time when the universe did not exist. Today it does. Some power from outside the universe must have caused this to happen. This is what we call God, the Creator.

The Entropy Argument

The generally accepted theory today is that the universe came into existence as a result of the Big Bang. We will discuss the Big Bang theory when we discuss the Free Lunch argument further; but suffice it to say here, that according to this theory, all matter and energy of our universe was once concentrated in a single massive object. The detonation of that object is referred to as the Big Bang. Immediately after the Big Bang, the universe consisted of sub-atomic particles flying around at speeds close to the speed of light and at very high temperatures.

The universe at this time must have been very disorderly. Scientists have a measure for the degree of 'disorderliness' of a system. It is known as Entropy; and it would have to be very high in the beginning of the universe. A law of Physics, called the Second Law of Thermodynamics says that the 'disorderliness' of a system can only increase over time, *unless external input has been applied to it.*

As an example, consider the apartment of a bachelor (who has a lot of clothes and dishes). From Monday through Saturday, the bachelor leaves home for work, comes back late, undresses and throws his clothes randomly in the room; orders food, and leaves the dishes and the debris lying around. His apartment gets more disorderly as the week progresses. Come Sunday, and his weekly maid comes to clean the apartment, does the dishes, washes, dries and irons the clothes and hangs them in the wardrobe. The 'disorderliness' suddenly reduces, but only because external effort (the maid) was applied.

Although many of us may be dissatisfied with the anarchical conditions that exist in our world today, to a physicist, the physical world is a lot smoother and more orderly than immediately after the Big Bang: its degree of 'disorderliness' has reduced considerably. The particles flying about haphazardly have settled down in the form of blocks of matter, called galaxies, solar systems and planets in an orderly fashion. This is in contradiction of the Second Law of Thermodynamics, unless an external input was applied. This, the argument says, was provided by God.

The Intelligent Design Argument

The universe seems to be run by certain laws of nature; and science has been trying to unravel them. But some entity must have laid down these laws, and ordered the nature to obey them. God?

These laws seem to have been very carefully 'designed'. If the laws weren't what they are, our world would not be what it is. If the apple, instead of falling straight on the ground below, were to wander around randomly, our universe would have been very different. Because the same laws that attract the apple to the ground, keep the Earth, moon and other planets in their proper positions.

The mathematical models of these laws often require arbitrary constants. For example, the law of gravitational attraction uses a constant **G**, and states that the force of attraction between two masses is equal to **G** times the product of the masses divided by the square of the distance separating them. This constant appears to be, at least so far, an arbitrary number, since it cannot be derived by any scientific reasoning or formula. It is also a *universal* constant, because its value does not change anywhere in the universe. Its value has also remained unchanged since the beginning of the universe, and will remain the same at all times in future. (The law of gravitation is itself a universal law, because it applies at all places and at all times within the universe). Now it is interesting to note that, although the value of **G** has been arbitrarily chosen 'by the nature', a different value of **G** would have made the universe unsustainable. A higher value would have increased the attraction between the masses so much that soon after the Big Bang, all particles would have fallen back on each other, and the universe would have collapsed. If the value of **G** had been too small, the force of attraction between masses would have been very feeble. The masses in the universe would then have flown away like dust particles, and not have formed larger bodies like the sun or planets. The same is the case with the other Universal Constants and parameters (and there are over 200 of them). Each constant must be within a tight band of values for the universe to exist. *Amazingly, every constant in our universe has been 'arbitrarily chosen' within this range!*

This leads one to believe that the universe has been 'designed' at the instant of the Big Bang (not earlier: Time did not exist before the Big Bang, as we will soon see). God played his role as the creator by intelligently designing the laws and the constants of the universe.

Science has answers to most of these questions today. Scientific research that has taken place since the last century has given rise to possibilities that did not exist earlier, and which lead to a conclusion that the universe had 'auto-bootstrapped' without the help of any external entity.

Here are the answers to the objections mentioned above.

Free Lunch and Big Bang

Scientists and philosophers have been pondering over the origin of the universe for many centuries. One of the theories which was popular for a long time was the Static Universe theory, which held that the universe has always been like it is now, and will always remain so in future. This theory was particularly popular with the scientific community, since most scientists felt uncomfortable with the idea of an external entity to have created the universe. According to the Static Universe theory, no matter how far back you went in time, the universe existed. There was never a time when there was no universe. Therefore, there was no question of its creation.

In 1915, Albert Einstein unraveled his masterpiece: The General Theory of Relativity. Four years later, a theoretical scientist, Alexander Friedmann, used this theory to trace the paths of all galaxies and stars of the universe *backwards in time*. He arrived at a surprising conclusion. When the paths of all bodies in the universe were traced backwards, they converged at a single point, in space and time. This implied that at one time, all matter in this universe was concentrated in a single, massive object, which has come to be known as the Cosmic Egg. About 13.7 billion years ago, the Cosmic Egg burst, spewing out all the matter it contained, in a phenomenon known as the Big Bang. The ramifications of this finding were shattering: It meant that the universe did not always look the way it appears today, and will probably look very different in the future. This dealt a body blow to the Static Universe theory. It meant that the universe *did* have a beginning and raised questions like what caused the Big Bang. It placed the Creator in limelight, as the One who lit the fuse.

Einstein, the scientist responsible for the General Theory of Relativity, was so distraught at the thought that his theory had resulted in the need to acknowledge a moment of creation, and hence the Creator, that he altered his theory and included certain arbitrary constants (known as Cosmological Constants) in his model, only to ensure that the paths of all matter, going back in time, did not converge.[6] But in 1929, an astronomer, Edwin Hubble, using a powerful telescope concluded that all galaxies are moving *away* from each other and the universe is actually expanding (in contradiction of the Static Universe Theory). This experimental observation confirmed the General Theory of Relativity in its original form, and Friedmann's thesis regarding the Cosmic Egg. The Static Universe Theory was scrapped, and the Big Bang model replaced it, leaving open uncomfortable questions like who (or what) caused the Big Bang.

Many theories have been offered since then which circumvent the need for a creator, but none was found satisfactory, until Stephen Hawking offered a brilliant scientific solution. Hawking had made notable contribution in our understanding of Black Holes, and had then turned his attention to the origin and the eventual fate of the universe.

Black Holes are formed when any mass in the universe is compressed under its own weight to an extent where its density, and consequently gravity are infinite. Stars which have turned into Black Holes are known to us — Black Holes are a reality and not a figment of imagination. The laws of science break down at Black Holes, because of the infinite density and gravitational attraction. Its large gravity allows it to collect any mass particle that comes

---

[6]   This, Einstein admitted later, was the first mistake that he had made. His second mistake, also in an effort to reject the possibility of forces unknown to science in the day-to-day life, was the rejection of the Uncertainty Principle of the Quantum Theory by saying '*God does not play dice*'. Quantum Theory also owes its development to Einstein's early work.

close to it; and nothing – not even light – is allowed to escape from it. Even time, which according to General Relativity slows down near very large masses, stands still in Black Holes. The Cosmic Egg, which contained all the mass that exists in the universe, was surely a Black Hole. It is therefore meaningless to talk about Time *during* the existence of the Cosmic Egg, or before that. If the Big Bang theory holds, Time started at the instant of the Big Bang. Of importance were the initial conditions of the universe at the time of the Big Bang, called the Boundary Conditions by scientists and mathematicians. The shape of the universe (including the value of the universal constants) would depend on what the initial conditions were. However, since all laws of science break down at the instant of the Big Bang, it is not possible to calculate backwards to arrive at the initial conditions.

Hawking postulated several hypotheses, which would have to be satisfied if the universe were to develop the way it has. As we have seen earlier, a hypothesis cannot be proven right: It is assumed correct unless proven wrong. Since his hypotheses answer all questions about the development of the universe so far, we have to accept the hypotheses to be true. It is likely that over the years, when we gather more knowledge, especially about how the two major theories discovered in the last century: General Relativity and Quantum Theory interact with each other; we would be able to disprove or further validate the hypotheses.

A detailed discussion of the hypotheses will involve too many scientific and mathematical descriptions, and is beyond the ambit of this book. I would therefore sum up this discussion by quoting from Hawking's book: *A Brief History of Time*:

> 'The idea that space and time may form a closed surface[7] without boundary also has profound implications for the role of God in affairs of the universe ... So long as the universe had a beginning, we could suppose it had a creator. But if the universe is completely self-contained, having no boundaries or edges, it would have neither beginning nor end: It would simply *be*. What place, then, for the creator?'

Disorderliness, Design and Anthropic Principle

Imagine a very large number of monkeys, each given a typewriter. If you can imagine a large enough number of monkeys, one of them would type out 'Romeo & Juliet'. How? Let us say that out of 100 monkeys, 99 have tossed their typewriters or played with them; the hundredth has hit the keyboard. Out of about 30 monkeys who have hit the keyboard, one will have hit the 'R' key. Out of the many who have hit 'R', nearly all would next do something meaningless with their typewriters, but one monkey would hit the 'o' key. And so on. If the number of monkeys is sufficiently large, it is possible to imagine that one of them

---

[7] According to one of the hypotheses, the universe is a closed surface in the space-time continuum, like our Earth is in the three dimensional space. We can keep going in one direction, without the possibility of falling off. The universe is thus, without any boundaries; and boundary conditions, which have been haunting scientists, do not apply.

will type out 'Romeo & Juliet' on his typewriter. This monkey may not be any more intelligent than his friend who is jumping up and down on his typewriter, but a series of accidents or chance events resulted in his having typed something meaningful. The monkey does not know that he has done anything which was considered impossible, and, (barring another improbable accident), will not be able to even remotely repeat his earlier act.

Mathematically, this is a case of multiplying a very small number by a very large number, to get a finite, non-zero result. Here, we have multiplied a very small probability (of a monkey accidentally pressing the right keys in the right sequence) by a very large number of monkeys, to each of whom this probability applies, to generate a finite number of times that this highly improbable event will occur. We will call a successful occurrence of the highly improbable event an 'accident'. When a person crosses a road, the probability that he would be hit by a car is insignificantly small. But with a very large number of persons crossing streets all the time, the number of times a car will hit a pedestrian (causing an accident in the conventional sense) is finite, in spite of the infinitesimal probability that each one has of getting run over.

When an 'accident' occurs, the entropy (or disorderliness) reduces, even if briefly, without any external effort, in an apparent contravention of the Second Law of Thermodynamics. Let us revert to the case of the bachelor's apartment and imagine a very large number of bachelors and their apartments. It may happen, that on one day (out of many, many days of their mundane routine), when one of those many, many bachelors tosses his shirt on a chair, the chair topples over, and as this happens, all the clothes on that chair fly across the room to the open wardrobe, and settle inside. (On hangers, if you like; only be prepared to imagine many more bachelors). Create a sequence of events, like we did in the case of the monkeys. Such an improbable event will also be an 'accident' and, of course, will require a large number of bachelors and a large observation period. This 'accident' will restore orderliness briefly, without expending any effort.

When we shuffle a deck of cards, we increase its disorderliness. (If the deck has already been shuffled, we may not increase the disorderliness much, but the Second Law of Thermodynamics will not allow it to reduce). And yet, cases have been reported of a Bridge game where the dealer has dealt a perfect hand (consisting of 13 cards of the same suit) to one of the players. Assuming that there was no trickery or practical joke, what has happened is that when the dealer shuffled the cards, they 'accidentally' assumed an order: Every fourth card was of the same suit. In fact, the probability of such an accident is not as low as in the earlier examples that we saw; and assuming that 5 million bridge-playing foursomes in the world play 20 hands everyday, 365 days a year, such an 'accident' could happen about once in 5 years.[8]

Do these examples mean that the Second Law of Thermodynamics is being violated? No. In a set of all possible disorderly sequences, there may be a few, very few, sequences with a semblance of orderliness. (For example,

---

[8] But a perfect *deal* (where all four players are dealt perfect hands) is more improbable (with odds of the order of 10^{-28}), and would take our 5 million bridge foursomes up to 5×10^{16} (5 followed by 16 zeroes) years! This is many times more than the age of our universe.

random numbers from 1 to 100,000 may contain a number like 12,345). The chances of our getting to a sequence like this may be very low, but with a large enough number of attempts, we may strike it accidentally. Like all accidents, this 'accident' is not deliberate, and cannot be replicated at will.

According to Hawking and other contemporary scientists, although there was chaos and disorderliness in a large number of areas in the early universe, it is possible that, given the vastness of the universe, there were a few areas which, by 'accident', were smooth and uniform. (This is like finding, in a well-shuffled pack of cards, **A**, **K** and **Q** of Hearts, for example, appearing together.) It was in these areas that particles started bonding to form nuclei of atoms, which then attracted electrons and formed atoms, the building blocks of matter. Blocks of this matter came together bonded by the gravitational attraction, and formed large bodies like galaxies, solar systems and planets.

How do we know that such events would have happened? *Because we are here, sitting on a planet, and thinking about the origin of the universe.* This is an example of the application of Anthropic Principle. This principle states that if the journey from the chaotic aftermath of the Big Bang to the present stage involving intelligent life on a planet required a few highly improbable events or 'accidents' to have taken place, they *must have* taken place at least once. Because without these 'accidents', we would not have existed. Our existence is proof enough that the 'accidents' had happened; no matter how improbable each of these 'accidents' may appear.

Another way of looking at the Anthropic Principle is: We see the universe the way it is, because we exist. In the words of Stephen Hawking:

> 'In a universe, vast in space-time, conditions for the development of intelligent life can be met only in certain regions which are limited in space and time. The intelligent beings in these regions should therefore not be surprised if they observe that their locality in the universe satisfies the conditions that are necessary for their existence.'

'Accidents' are necessary for the application of the Anthropic Principle. Very rare occurrences of smooth space-time, combined with the large amount of space-time available in the universe caused the early building blocks to develop. If the region where the developments were taking place was not suitable for sustaining the development, (for example, if the gravitational law did not exist, or a fundamental constant was outside its acceptable range), the building blocks in that region fell apart, till the next 'accident' happened. The Anthropic Principle argues that we could only be discussing these questions in a universe that was capable of producing us. Our existence here determines that all conditions necessary for intelligent life exist in the region of the universe we are in.

An alternative hypothesis explaining the development of the universe suggests that there are *many* universes, like bubbles of foam. The laws of science and the constants are specific to each universe. The Anthropic Principle comes into play to explain that we must be in one of the rare universes, where, by 'accident', the laws and constants happen to be favorable to our eventual evolution and hence contemplation of the problem.

To a theist, Anthropic Principle is hard to swallow. But as Richard Dawkins, a confirmed atheist puts it:

> 'The theist says that God, when setting up the universe, tuned the fundamental constants of the universe so that each one lay within the acceptable zone for the production of life. It is as though God had a number of knobs that he could twiddle, and he carefully tuned each knob to the acceptable value. As ever, the theist's answer is deeply unsatisfying, because it leaves the existence of God unexplained. A God capable of calculating the acceptable values of the fundamental constants would have to be at least as improbable, as the finely tuned combination of the numbers itself, and that's very improbable indeed ... (Such a God) must be a supremely complex and improbable entity who needs an even bigger explanation than the one he is supposed to provide.'

In summary, scientific discoveries in all disciplines of science have taken away from God responsibilities that were once associated with Him: not only the administration of the world, but also the creation of the universe. Very strong theories and hypotheses that have been formulated on the strength of recent scientific discoveries, suggest that the universe has been self-created and self-administered, without God.

4

FROM DARWIN TO DNA

Zindagi ittefaq hai
(Life is an 'Accident')

- Sahir Ludhianvi

If the creation of universe appears, to some people, to be an act of Intelligent Design, so does the creation of life on Earth, so wonderfully tailored to meet the requirements specific to each species. This is the third role that people assign to God.

Several questions arise in the context of life on Earth. Some of them are: (1) Are we alone in this universe? (2) What created the spark of life on Earth? (3) Why do plants, animals and humans appear so well designed?

Anybody Out There?

Unlike the geocentric model of Aristotle and Ptolemy of about 2000 years ago, which placed the Earth in the center of the universe, and the heliocentric model of Copernicus and Galileo, which assumed the Sun to be the center of our existence, we now know that Earth is a medium-sized planet, orbiting around a medium-sized sun, which is a part of an ordinary galaxy, called the Milky Way. There are about 10^{20} or so planets in this universe, and Earth is not a special planet.

But Earth *is* special in one way: It is bio-friendly. It has the necessary conditions to support life.[9] Liquid water is available on the planet, as also an atmosphere that contains oxygen: both essential for our kind of life. The orbit around sun is elliptical (giving us a variety of climatic conditions), but not too elliptical. Thus the temperature at any point and at all times on Earth is within acceptable limits.

Do other planets in our solar system (or their satellites) offer similar bio-friendly atmosphere? Moon, the only object in the outer space that we have visited[10], has no atmosphere, so life would not survive there. There are three main candidates in our solar system, according to BBC, which can harbor life: Mars, Europa and Titan. Over the next decades, space probes will be sent to them. Mars is most similar to Earth, but has now become too cold for life to exist there. But primitive organisms may have thrived there in the past. Europa is one of Jupiter's satellites. The surface temperature is a chilly -170° C. But this inhospitable satellite may harbor an underground ocean of liquid water — one of the essential ingredients for life. Titan is the largest moon of

---

[9]   'Life', here, refers to the life forms whose bio-chemistry is not unimaginably different from what we see on the Earth. Life forms that would freeze to death at 25° C, and would need a jacket when the temperature drops below 500° C; or inhale Hydrogen Sulfide for healthy living and choke on Oxygen, are in the domain of science fiction writers.

[10]   These comments are based on the current situation. Man may land on Mars soon, and what we know about the planet could get revised then.

Saturn, and the only moon in the Solar System with a dense atmosphere. The atmosphere on Titan could be identical to that of the early Earth when life began. The orange haze surrounding the globe could conceal carbon-rich lakes, oceans and storms of chemical rain. Could it also house life?

Our solar system may be the only hope that we can have to meet the Little Green Men. The nearest solar system is about 4 light years away, and the distances to some of the other solar systems within our galaxy would run into millions of light years. NASA is trying to systematically look for Earth-type planets by trying to analyze light received from 100,000 stars, which may have been emitted from those stars millions of years ago. Going to any planet of these solar systems is out of the question, but even sending messages to them may also be almost impossible. As no electromagnetic wave travels faster than light, it would take millions of years for any message to reach there. There would also be the question of language. The life on the planets that we send the message to would have to be intelligent enough not only to receive and decode our message, but also to transmit the reply to us. And if the reply is 'Pardon …?', the person on the Earth who receives this reply may be a million years younger than the person who transmitted the question!

Since we would never be interacting with any aliens from outside our solar system, we are left with statistical techniques to determine whether or not there is life on those planets. Given that there are about 10^{20} planets in the universe, even a negligible probability of, say, one planet in a hundred billion being bio-friendly, could mean that there are one billion planets in the universe, which have the conditions necessary to host life. We can recognize this situation as something that we had encountered in the last chapter: A very small probability, and a very large population. The Anthropic Principle comes to our help here also. We may still not have any clue where the other one billion life-supporting planets are, but the Anthropic Principle tells us that we know of at least one of them: Because we are living on it.

Beginning of Life on Earth

Cell is the basic building block in all living matter; and DNA is an important molecule in the cell. We will discuss DNA later, but suffice it to say here, that DNA has an interesting property of self-replication. DNA also holds some information in the form of a blueprint for the development of the cell and the organism that the cell belongs to. When the DNA is replicated, this information is also copied in the replica. Research chemists have been attempting to produce DNA in their laboratories, but so far without success. The chemical reactions required for this molecule apparently cannot take place, until certain specific atmospheric conditions are maintained. Scientists have tried many different combinations of atmospheric conditions, but so far, none has catalyzed the chemical reaction. There is once again, an argument in favor of an external creator: that God has created life, and no laboratory in the world has been able to emulate that action. But if you realize that Earth had been in existence for a few billion years before life sprouted on it for the first time, that it had experienced some vicious changes in atmospheric conditions during this period, and that all elements required for the chemical reactions to produce a DNA molecule were available in the environment, there is once again a case for applying the Anthropic Principle. Remember that just a single molecule of DNA can account for all the life that we see on Earth today, because DNA can replicate itself. Given the vast opportunities available, the improbable event of having just the right environmental conditions required to produce DNA could have been accomplished 'accidentally' at least once. In fact, we *know* that it was accomplished, because we are here.

The Design Argument

When we see a seagull, flying several meters above the sea, spot its culinary delight in the waters below, plunge down, pick up its prey in a single attempt and soar back in the sky, we cannot but wonder about the way its eyes, wings and beak have been 'designed'. Our human eyes, also very complex in design, do not have the capability that the gulls' eyes have; but they serve our purpose very well (unless they malfunction). We also don't have beaks and wings, but then, we do not need them. Our bodies are 'designed' to carry out their functions with the organs that we are fitted with. Butterflies' wings are very delicate compared to gulls', but they are 'designed' for a different purpose. They are light enough to make them flit from one flower to another, and have a bright design on them, which is their defense mechanism against predators.

This 'design' argument applies to all species that we see on Earth, and to each of their organs. The argument suggests that all life forms and their organs have been carefully and painstakingly 'designed' by the One who created life on this planet. We have hands so that we can work. Elephants have trunks for the kind of work that they need to do. Flowers are brightly colored so that they can attract bees and butterflies for pollination. Leaves are green to perform photosynthesis (a very complex process involving about 70 different chemical reactions).

Can the Anthropic Principle answer the Design Argument as well? The answer is an emphatic NO. It is too much to expect that fortuitous 'accidents' can explain the way the 10 million or so species that exist on our planet today happen to be fitted to their specific ways of life. The origin of life was a unique event that had to happen only once (as also the origin of the universe that we saw in the last chapter). But the luxuriant diversity in life that we observe around us has to have some other explanation. New species keep appearing on Earth; and if we could see the life on Earth after a thousand years, we would see yet unknown species, well adapted to their environment. Unlike the origin of life, here we are faced with the possibility of a continual tinkering with the species to adapt them to the constantly changing environment.

Before Charles Darwin came on the scene, there was a general agreement that God designed each species to fit its environment. This would mean that God was intervening continuously, tinkering with the life forms, adding some new ones, and modifying others to suit the environment. Darwin changed that belief with his theory of Natural Selection.

Evolution and the Principle of Natural Selection

Till the end of 18th century, the western world still thought that the age of Earth was no more than 6000 years. With such a short time span, Earth was believed to be unchanging. This belief received a jolt when, in the late 18th century, William Smith, a miner, made the first systematic study of fossils and the different strata of rocks that they were embedded in. This study suggested that Earth was much older than they had imagined. With time, new strata were laid down one on top of another. During the different periods of time, different life forms had appeared, living on Earth for a time, only to be replaced by others.

These ideas were incorporated into a theory, which believed that the total time span of the earth was divided into epochs; each epoch had its own life forms and ended with a catastrophe sent by God. After each such upheaval, new life forms were specially created by God, adapted to the new conditions on Earth, and were destroyed in the next catastrophe.

In the early 19th century, James Hutton and Lyell, both geologists, concluded that a sudden catastrophe was not necessary to explain the formation of the various strata, but the effects of natural processes that operate on Earth even today – such as soil erosion, earthquakes and volcanic activities – were sufficient to explain the changes that had taken place in Earth's surface since it was first formed, provided these natural processes had sufficient time span to work with. The extinction of various species was now seen to be the consequence of the changing conditions on Earth which destroyed the ecological niche to which the species were adapted. No explanation was offered for where the new life forms came from to fit the new ecological niches created when the conditions changed. There was still a role for God, in the early 19th century: not just a once and for all creation of life, but day to day tinkering to ensure the right species in the right ecological niche.

Charles Darwin, a British naturalist, sailed on *HMS Beagle* as the captain's mate to chart the coastline of South America in 1831. In the Galapagos Archipelago, off the coast of Ecuador in the Pacific Ocean, he observed the different species of birds on different islands and noted the similarities and differences in them. He attributed similarities to the descent from a common ancestor — a species from the mainland; and the differences to the exquisite tailoring to fit the different ecologies of different islands. However, he was unsure of the mechanism through which descendants were gradually modified into forms different from the ancestors, and best suited for their ecological niche.

Darwin's ideas were influenced by the famous *Essay on the Principle of Population* (1838) by Thomas Malthus. He had pointed out that many more individuals of each species are born than can possibly survive; and consequently, there is a frequently recurring struggle for existence. Darwin theorized that the least well adapted individuals within a species would be losers in the struggle for limited resources and those which are best fitted to their niches would survive and procreate. This theory is famously called the Survival of the Fittest.

Darwin likened this process occurring in nature with the breeding of domesticated animals (dogs, horses), where the breeder would cull newborn animals that did not conform to his requirements, and nurture the ones that did. Nature could do the same trick, by choosing the individuals best suited for a particular niche, and leaving the others to die. This he called Natural Selection.

Darwin reasoned that Natural Selection could work with variations that arose accidentally. If it happened that a bird on an island was born with a slightly longer beak, *and if that helped to find food*, there was every chance that it would survive, and reproduce to pass on the characteristic long beak to its off-springs. Birds with shorter beaks would be progressively squeezed out of that particular niche, because birds with long beaks would eat all the food. If on another island, a thick, short beak were an advantage, (because, say, the main food on that island was worms crawling on the ground), then over many generations, the descendants of the original settlers would evolve with thick, short beaks. In due course, the two families of birds, descended originally from identical ancestors would become quite distinct. This process operating over a long enough timescale could explain not only the differences between closely related species, but also between lion and tiger, man and ape, and all other species of plants and animals on Earth. Given the long timescale provided by the understanding of geology prevailing in the 19th century, the accidental variations among individuals was all that Darwin needed to explain the evolution of all species from the original primordial living cell.

John Gribbin, in his book 'In Search of the Double Helix' summarizes the three keys to Darwin's theory of evolution:

> It operates on individuals within the species, allowing only the fittest to survive.

> It involves inherited characteristics, which
> are passed from one generation to the next.
>
> The process of inheritance is imperfect, so
> that nature has a variety in each generation
> to practice the process of selection.

Darwin's theory of Natural Selection not only explains how the life forms have evolved so far, but will also apply to the future evolution. Global warming is an ecological concern of the world today. Whilst all efforts to reduce carbon emissions and global warming must be applauded, the Principle of Natural Selection will ensure that, over a long period of time, all species – plants, animals and humans – will gradually adapt to the ecological changes brought about by global warming. Off-springs from each species that are more tolerant to the new ecology will live longer, and reproduce; while those who are not equipped to deal with the effects of global warming will die sooner, and will not procreate. Species that do not or cannot introduce the variability to face the new challenge will be eradicated (as dinosaurs were). Over a long period of time, when the ecology has changed, the species that populate Earth will be optimally fitted to the new ecology.

Darwin's theory of evolution was not very easily accepted. But the reasons for rejecting it were mainly religious: The theory went against the accepted belief that God created each species Himself. (The chauvinists refused to believe that the human race was not the exquisite creation of God Himself, but was descended from apes!) When it was postulated, Natural Selection was only a theory – brilliant and unique, but abstract and without a concrete explanation for how the characteristics of a species were transmitted to the off-springs, and how, variability was introduced, which became the criterion for Natural Selection. But the amazing thing about this remarkably deep insight is that over the next one and a half century, the development of genetics and discovery of DNA proved Darwin right again and again on virtually every count. Most of the scientific community now accepts the principle of Natural Selection.

Anthropic Principle and Natural Selection complement each other. Anthropic Principle is applicable in one-off situations, where highly improbable events have a very large opportunity to happen. If the event happens, it is by an 'accident', but if such an event is a necessary condition for the presence of intelligent life in the universe (or on Earth), we *know* the accident had occurred[11]. Natural Selection, on the other hand does not depend on an accident. It is an ongoing process of adaptively fitting the species to the changing environment. The statistical improbability that we see in the apparent design in the living creatures is explained by slow and gradual evolution from a simple beginning.

---

[11]   'Intelligent', 'Life' and 'universe' / 'Earth' are all important. In the last chapter, we saw the Cosmological application of this principle. In this chapter, we saw its application in the origin of life. The origin of intelligence and consciousness also requires an improbable leap from mere life, and this is attributed to eukaryotic cells (ones with a nucleus unlike the prokaryotic cells of bacteria). This is a one-off event, and not a gradual biological adaptation, and can be explained by the Anthropic argument that out of the billion planets with life at the level of bacteria, a fraction of the life forms made it to the higher level with eukaryotic cells. And we are a testimony to this.

Genes

The first hint of how species transmit their characteristics to their off-springs came around 1856, when a German-Czech monk, Gregor Mendel experimented with peas. He was not a scientist by training or by vocation. But he had the curiosity of a scientist, a desire to satisfy his curiosity through experimental methods and the ability to think outside the box while interpreting the results of his experiments. He took pure-bred plants: some which always produced green peas and some which produced yellow peas; and cross-fertilized them. The first generation offspring produced peas, which were yellow. Then these first-generation cross-bred peas were planted and were allowed to fertilize themselves naturally. In this second generation, about ¾ of the peas were yellow and ¼ green.

Based on these observations and the work on other characteristics he studied, he came up with a simple explanation. Each property ('yellowness' or 'greenness', in our example) corresponds to what we now call a gene. Genes are carried in a *double-dose* in each pea. One form of the gene, called dominant gene, dominates over the other (the latter called recessive). In the peas that Mandel experimented with, 'yellowness' was the dominant gene, and 'greenness' was the recessive gene. Today these variations of the same gene are called *alleles*. If we call the allele for yellow **A** and the allele for green **a,** then a pure bred yellow pea would be **AA**, and a pure bred green pea would be **aa**. When they are crossed the peas produced will inherit one allele from each parent. The first generation peas would therefore be **Aa** (and not **aA** – by convention, the dominant gene is mentioned first). They are yellow, the character dictated by the dominant gene.

Now when these hybrids (*Aa*) are allowed to fertilize themselves, every new plant will inherit one allele from each parent. Half the time it inherits *A* from one parent and *a* from another, and is *Aa* (yellow). One quarter of the time it inherits *A* from both parents and is *AA* (yellow), and another quarter of the time it inherits *a* from both parents and is *aa* (green). So in the second generation, ¾ of the peas are yellow and ¼ are green.

Of the two alleles of each gene present in the individual, only the dominant one determines the physical structure of the organism. This important point distinguishes between the genotype, or the "blueprint" of the instructions carried by the genetic material, and the phenotype, or the overall physical appearance of the individual. Peas with a green phenotype always have only one genotype: *aa*; whereas Peas with a yellow phenotype may have one of two different genotypes: *AA* or *Aa*.

Mendel noted an important exception to the rule about each gene being carried in a double dose. When sexual organisms reproduce, the gametes (pollen and seed in plants, sperm and egg in animals) contain a *single set of genes*, with one allele in the parents' genotype being segregated at random. The *fertilized egg* thereby contains a full double complement of genes, one set inherited from each parent. But the resulting genotype need not be (and in practice will not be) identical to either parent.

In spite of Mendel's pioneering work in determining rules of heredity, 'genes' were still an abstract concept, and scientists did not know which molecules in the body were responsible for transmitting their traits to the next generation. But Mendel had laid a strong foundation for further research in Genetics, which continued to surprise the world as the mystery of life was unraveled, bit by bit, in the next decades.

Cells and Chromosomes

Cells are the smallest independent parts of organisms: they are the building blocks of life. The human body contains about 100 trillion cells, give or take a few trillion; while very small organisms like bacteria are just a single cell.

Cells multiply by dividing into two[12], with each divided cell growing independently. This process of cell division is called mitosis. A cell continually absorbs materials from the environment, processes them into its structure and grows to a certain size, after which it divides into two, and the two identical daughter cells repeat the cycle. The process of cell division is used to grow the organism and to repair damage in worn out tissues.

If you look at a human cell under the microscope, the nucleus, the largest structure in the cell, is easily visible. It is surrounded by the nuclear membrane, and contains certain thread-like structures. These are called chromosomes. Chromosomes contain proteins and nucleic acids. They are always present in pairs, which are dissimilar. (Humans have 23 pairs of chromosomes). During mitosis, this pair gets duplicated, and a nuclear membrane forms around each set of chromosomes as the cell splits across the middle. The resulting two cells each have a complete set of chromosomes

---

[12]   Mathematicians, don't frown at this sentence!

identical to those of the original cell, and it is impossible to say which of the two cells is original and which a copy.

There is also another form of cell division. The cell division of germ cells (sperms and eggs in animals) is different, and is called meiosis. The crucial difference between mitosis and meiosis is that mitosis makes exact copies of cells with a full complement of paired chromosomes (diploid cells), but meiosis produces cells which contain only one chromosome of each type (haploid cells). Since each haploid cell contains, at random, one chromosome from each pair in the original cell, the haploid cells produced by meiosis are not identical.[13] The fertilized egg, produced when two haploid cells (the egg and the sperm) fuse together has a full double complement of chromosomes. Although each of the 46 chromosomes in the human fertilized egg can be traced back to either the egg or the sperm, the fertilized egg is different from the cells of either parent.

This discovery has a remarkable resemblance with Mendel's findings. In each chromosome pair in an individual, one member originally comes from the mother and the other from the father, though each has been faithfully copied several times during mitosis since the egg had been fertilized. Genes are strung along the chromosomes. Any gene which exists in the cell of any human being can be expressed in an individual phenotype in the next generation: any one of the two alleles carried by a woman may be paired in her children with any one of the two alleles of the same gene carried by a man. This gives an idea of the potential that exists for the variety of genotype for the next generation. (Each human

---

[13]   Each human (male or female) with 23 pairs of chromosomes can produce 2^{23} or 8 million different haploid cells.

couple can produce 2^{23} x 2^{23} genetically distinct entities). The entire range of alleles is called the gene pool. It is from this large gene pool, that natural selection decides which alleles will stay in the pool and which will disappear.[14]

Sometimes, during the process of cell division, one or more genes on a chromosome exchange places with equivalent genes carried by the chromosome's paired partner. This process is called recombination. Sometimes other errors in copying genetic information (mutations) take place. If this happens during mitosis, the result is not very significant, as these changes are not passed on to the next generation. But if this happens during meiosis, a different genotype is created. Recombination and mutation result in a constant reshuffling of the genetic pack that gives the variety for the natural selection to operate on.

Experimental evidence exists to show that only those traits which are genetically coded are transmitted to the off-springs; acquired traits are not. Does a musician's son have an edge over others in becoming a good musician? The father's musical abilities would be partly due to his own genes, and partly acquired through training and practice. The genes accounting for his musical abilities could be

---

[14] Out of all pairs of chromosomes, one pair is of particular importance. All chromosomes look similar under the microscope; this pair looks different between the males and the females. One member of this pair called **X**, because of its shape is present in both, but the other member is an **X** or a **Y** depending on the sex. In humans, females carry **XX** and the males carry **XY**. After meiosis, the egg will always carry **X** as the 23rd chromosome in humans, but the sperm may carry either **X** or **Y**. *Thus the sex of the offspring is determined by the sperm.* This could be an eye-opener for those husbands who banish their wives for not giving them sons. The wives are not at fault: their own sperms are of the 'wrong' kind.

passed on to the son, if the sperm which was successful at the time of his conception had the right chromosomes. If his wife also had it in her genes to be musically inclined, it would increase the chances that the son would inherit music from the parents. But the musical abilities *acquired* by the father will not pass to the son – he would have to train and practice; and acquire this talent on his own. The atmosphere of music in the family may help, but still, the son will not inherit the acquired talents of his parents.

DNA

Although the study of cells and chromosomes showed the promise of providing answers to the mystery of inheritance and variability, the gene continued to be an illusive concept. Scientists had theorized that there existed a genetic code, stored in the cell, which provided a blueprint for the development of the individual right from the embryonic stage. The code would copy itself each time the cell is divided. Such a code would be translated by the cells to produce different types of proteins, which govern the development of the cell and the organism as a whole.[15] In a human body, for instance, the genetic code would determine the color of the eyes, the shape of the nose; and build the machinery that is the human body. Parts of this code would come from either parent. Similarly, parts of the code would be transmitted to the offspring.

Chromosomes, given the role they play in mitosis and meiosis, were the obvious place for the scientists to look for

---

[15]   Ribonucleic Acid (RNA) is known to function as a carrier of genetic information and a catalyst of biochemical reactions and protein synthesis.

the genetic code. But chromosomes contain protein and DNA (deoxyribonucleic acid); and scientists did not know which of these is responsible for inheritance.

Proteins are made of Amino Acids. Very many amino acids can exist in principle, many have been made in the lab; and 20 are found in proteins. DNA, on the other hand, is a double-stranded molecule that is twisted into a helix like a spiral staircase. Each strand is comprised of a sugar-phosphate backbone and some base chemicals. The four bases that make up the stairs in the spiraling staircase are adenine (A), thymine (T), cytosine (C) and guanine (G).

Although as early as in 1884, microscopic observations during fertilization of an egg had suggested that DNA was the chemical which played a role in the fertilization, attention of those working on heredity was initially drawn towards proteins, which by virtue of the fact that 20 different amino acids were a more likely and efficient candidate to store the code of life than the DNA with only 4 variables.

It was James Watson and Francis Crick who, in 1953, determined the double helical structure of DNA and showed that this double helix with the four bases inside held the genetic code. The bases have an important property. A and T form a complementary pair, and have a tendency to form hydrogen bonds. Similarly G and C pair together. This property of complementary base pairing has two important ramifications in the Watson - Crick Model of DNA as a double helix. First, any sequence of base pairs along the helix can be accommodated by the structure. Looking at just one strand of the helix, there is no restriction on the sequence of the 4 base 'letters' A, C, G and T. The complementary strand mirrors whatever letters the first strand carries, (if the first carries A, the second T and *vice versa*; similarly, if the first carries G, the second C and *vice versa*). So it is the sequence along one strand that matters, and there is complete freedom of any 'message' of any length to be written in a four-letter code. And second, it provides for easy replication. Before this idea was put forward, it was believed that replication was always a two-step process. First, the molecule would have to create an intermediate form, a 'negative'. Then the negative would be used to create a new molecule. The double-stranded structure of DNA, with complementary bases paired along the length of the molecule meant that it carried its own 'negative'. Once the original chain is unwound, there would be no difficulty in assembling a new chain to partner each of the single strands, pairing up the appropriate base at each point along each single chain (A with T, C with G) to create a new complementary strand, producing two double strands of DNA where only one existed before.

The Watson - Crick Model marked the beginning of a new era in genetic biology that allowed scientists to study the details of heredity at the *molecular level*. Today, more than 60 years later, tremendous progress has been made owing to this path-breaking concept; and thousands of scientists are looking for new horizons in the genetic technology.

To summarize, life was started by an accident. But after the first living cell was created, it multiplied, and evolved, over billions of years into the variety of life forms that we see on Earth today. The manner in which cells can self-replicate, preserving the genetic code; the way the genetic material guides the development of the organism as laid down in the genetic code; the special treatment given to the germ cells and how germ cells from two different organisms can combine to form a new cell, unlike either of the parent cells but with traits inherited from both; and how mutations can result in an infinite variety of alleles, from which the fittest survive the changing environment: all account for the 'design' that we see in living forms on Earth. And all of this has been tested: not only in laboratories but also in live situations. Life has been created and is going on, without a role for God.

5

BODY AND SOUL

Cogito, ergo sum
(I think, therefore I am)

-René Descartes

Personal God

We saw in the earlier chapters, that sufficient scientific evidence has now emerged for the rational and science-minded people to accept that our universe was created and is run without God. And that life was created on Earth and different life forms have emerged on their own, without God. The concept of God was Man's creation, and in the dark ages, before science, it was inevitable that Man should create God. After all, many questions could not be answered then, without invoking God: how does the sun rise in the east every morning, who drags it across the sky to the other end, who causes rain, river flow, ocean tides, volcanic eruptions or earthquakes? God became the answer to all of these questions. Later, when Man wondered about the creation of the universe, the life on this planet and the exquisite manner in which each life form is fitted with what is needed for it to survive; the concept of God was enlarged to answer these questions as well.

Those who accept, in the face of scientific discoveries from gravity to Higg's boson, that God is an inevitable, but a man-made concept, and does not have to exist to explain the existence of universe or life on Earth, are now faced with an important question to answer. *Is there a God that plays a role in the personal life of every individual?* Is there a Personal God for each individual to talk to, to pray to, to thank and to apologize to? Someone who keeps every individual under observation, and metes out rewards and punishments depending on their deeds?

Consistent with the earlier notion about God, it was possible to imagine that this omnipresent, omnipotent, and omniscient entity also takes minute to minute decisions about events in our lives. Those who have ever prayed for the recovery of an ill family member, or before an important event in their lives, have tacitly accepted that the entity they are praying to exists, and can decide the course of events in their lives. But when we have deleted God from all other explanations, is it rational to still believe in an entity that micro-manages the lives of all individuals on Earth (and God alone knows on how many other planets)? If we agree that it was a mistake (though an inevitable one, in the absence of science) to create the idea of God for everything that we now know happens without any external influence, then could it also be a mistake to attribute the happenings in our personal lives to God?

In the earlier chapters, I have argued against the existence of God in the role of an administrator or of a creator of the universe and of life. I am now going to *assume*, that God does not exist in the role of a Personal God; and will try and describe how the world and our lives go on without 'somebody up there' who listens to our prayers and intervenes in our lives. Even rational people, who have understood and accepted the ramifications of the scientific discoveries, may find it difficult to accept that their lives, and indeed lives of all others, are run without any external force. It requires a change in the paradigm to believe that in this World without God, everything that happens to them and around them *just happens*, without it being pre-ordained, or being a part of a complex conspiracy by an unknown entity for an unknown purpose.

Personal God is about *human* prayers, *human* sins, *human* atonement, *human* aspirations and *human* fears. I will, therefore, confine the discussion on Personal God only to human beings.

Life is Chemistry

When the first child is born to a couple, it is not unusual for the couple to wonder, or even openly express that it is miraculous that they were able to create something out of nothing, and that the 'something' looks so similar to them. But based on what we saw in the last chapter, 'creation' of a child is no more miraculous than throwing up a ball, and watching it come down. There are, of course, different emotions involved in seeing your own child and seeing a ball obey the law of gravitation; but the child-birth that gives people a feeling of miracles also follows laws, which biological research has discovered. From the moment the egg in the woman's womb is fertilized, it is a living cell, which will multiply, according to a genetic code, or a blueprint which is stored in the cell itself. And each parent has contributed to the blueprint. It is no surprise that the foetus grows to develop human features (it *would* be a miracle, if it developed a tail or horns), with likeness to its parents. The blueprint directs the cells to produce specific proteins and enzymes out of the organic substances around it and guides the development of the organism, not only inside the womb, but for the rest of its life. The facial features, height and other physiognomic aspects, aptitudes and susceptibility to specific diseases are all a part of that blueprint. Human body is chemistry. Life – the self-replication of cells according to a genetic code – is also chemistry. God has not given us life.

Darwin's principle of Natural Selection has ensured that there is an organ in the human anatomy for everything that we need to do. The principle also ensures economy of design: no organism gets organs which are redundant. So every organ in our body has a function to perform. For example, blood circulates throughout the body and supplies oxygen to all parts. The waste matter that blood collects *en route* gets filtered in the kidneys. De-oxidized blood comes to the lungs for oxidation. And so on. Heart is an important part of the anatomy, because it pumps the oxidized blood throughout the body, and collects de-oxidized blood for sending it to the lungs. Malfunction of the heart may reduce or stop the blood flow to all organs, and can cause serious problems in their functioning.

But the most important, and also the most complex organ in the human body is the brain. It receives sensory inputs from the spinal cord and sensory organs such as eyes and ears; processes these inputs and initiates appropriate and coordinated motor actions. It is the center for all vital body activities, and controls body temperature, blood pressure, heart rate and breathing. It performs executive functions like planning and problem solving. It provides the language ability, unique to human brains. It has a memory, which it manages by storing information, recalling it and using it in its other functions such as decision making.

During the initial stages of computer design, people took the human brain as a model and created the architecture of the computer to imitate the processes in a human brain. Now that computers have become ubiquitous, it may be easier to understand the processes in human brains by comparing them with computers.

The brain is made of billions of nerve cells, called neurons. Neurons are comparable to the electronic gates and wires in a computer. They have the ability to gather and transmit electrochemical signals over long distances, up to several feet, and pass messages to each other. Chemical and electrical synapses are specialized junctions through which neurons signal to each other and to non-neuronal cells such as those in muscles. Synapses allow neurons to form circuits within the central nervous system. Unlike a computer, where signals are electronic impulses, the brain uses chemical and electrical signals.

Different parts of the brain carry out the tasks of the Input and Output units, the Central Processing Unit (CPU) and the memory in a computer.

Let us see in some detail, how the human memory functions.

Human Brain and Memory

The sound of your mother's lullaby, the taste of your favorite home-cooked sweet, the scent of the soil after the first shower. These are memories that make up the ongoing experience of your life — they provide you with a sense of self. They are what makes you feel comfortable with familiar people and surroundings, ties your past with your present, and provides a framework for the future. In a profound way, it is our collective set of memories that makes us who we are.

Human memory is much more complex and elusive than the way memory is structured in a computer. It is not located in one particular part in the brain but is instead a brain-wide process. If you think of an object, say, a rose, your brain retrieves the object's name, its shape, its scent, its color, the softness of its petals, the sharpness of its thorns from different regions of the brain. The entire image of the 'rose' is actively reconstructed by the brain from many different areas. Yet you are never aware of these separate mental experiences, nor that they are all coming from different parts of your brain, because they all work together.

The creation of a memory begins with its perception. The perception is encoded before it is stored in the memory using the language of electricity and chemistry. All the action in the brain occurs at the synapses, where electrical pulses carrying messages leap across gaps between cells.

Memory passes through three stages of filtration. The first is the sensory stage; then the short-term memory; and ultimately, for some memories, the long-term memory. This scheme provides a means to screen different memories, and store in the brain only what needs to be stored. When I drove to work, I had the habit of reading the license plate number of the car in front of me. But if each number I read had stayed in my memory for a long time, my brain would have collapsed under the burden of the information it has stored.

The registration of information during perception occurs in the brief sensory stage that usually lasts only a fraction of a second. It is your sensory memory that allows a perception such as a visual pattern, a sound, or a touch to linger for a brief moment after the stimulation is over.

After that first flicker, the sensation is stored in short-term memory. Short-term memory has a fairly limited capacity; it can hold only a few items for no more than 20 or 30 seconds at a time. It is this short-term memory that allows you to 'remember' the 10-digit telephone number that you looked up in the telephone directory, till you have dialed it.

Important information is gradually transferred from short-term memory into long-term memory. The more the information is repeated or used, the more likely it is to eventually end up in long-term memory, or be 'retained.' Unlike sensory and short-term memory, which are limited and decay rapidly, long-term memory can store unlimited amounts of information indefinitely. Experts suggest that unless the brain is damaged, nothing in the long-term memory is ever forgotten — only the means of retrieving it is sometimes lost.

When most people refer to memory, they refer only to long term memory.

When you want to remember something, you retrieve the information on an unconscious level, bringing it into your conscious mind at will. Sometimes a memory cannot be retrieved - a phenomenon you might call 'forgetting'. If you have forgotten something, it may be because you did not encode it very effectively, or because you were distracted while encoding should have taken place, or because you are having trouble retrieving it. For example, do you remember whose face appears on the currency note that you use to make your daily purchases? If you don't, you have not really encoded its appearance, so that if you tried to describe it, you probably couldn't. Distractions that occur while you are trying to remember something can get in the way of encoding memories. When you are late to leave home for work, and your wife gives you instructions on what to bring on your way back home, you may forget these instructions, because you had not effectively saved them in your memory. You may also forget because you are simply having trouble retrieving the memory. Retrieval of memory is eased by cues and mood. If you have ever tried to recall something and could not, but then later it came to you in a flash, it could be because there was a mismatch between retrieval cues and the encoding of the information; and the right cues and mood helped you retrieve it later. Old and forgotten sights, sound of a favorite piece of music and similar cues can involuntarily revive memories of times associated with the cues.

Brain and Mind

The human brain is an organ of soft tissue that fills the skull. Mind, on the other hand, is an abstract space, where reality of the world, including oneself, as perceived by the individual is mirrored. It is the faculty of consciousness and thought. It is the element of a person that enables them to be aware of the world and their experiences in it. It is the feeling of 'being me now'. It is what the spiritualists call 'the soul' or *chitta*.

Consciousness is by definition a private experience; accessible only to the person it belongs to, unlike other physical phenomena. For example: Do you see the same red that I see? A red object reflects light of a wave-length of 600 nanometers. This light creates an image on the retina, which is transmitted by optic nerves to the part of the brain that has to do with vision. So far, what has happened is physical, and unless you are color blind, there will be no difference in the signals that reach your brain and mine. However, there is no way to compare the *feeling* of the red color that will be generated in our minds. Neither of us would be able to describe our perception of the color that we have felt, except by referring to other red objects like blood or post box. But whilst we will both agree that blood and post boxes are red, because they match the color that each of us individually knows as red, we could still be having different experiences. This applies to all perceptions, feelings and emotions. Two patients sitting in dentist's chairs may suffer pain, when the dentist is drilling. Each may react to pain in a similar fashion, like contort the face, squirm and occasionally let out a sound. And yet, neither of them would be able to describe their feeling of pain (and not because of language or articulation problems – or because it is difficult to speak with a drill in your mouth). Your mind is your own: not even your mother can know what happens in that abstract space.

Daniel Dennet, American philosopher, who has done considerable research on the philosophy of mind, explains that human consciousness is an experience of three kinds of phenomena: [1] experiences of the 'external' world – sights, sound, smells, textures etc; [2] experiences of the internal world – ideas, recollections, fantasy, images, daydreaming; and [3] experiences of emotion – pain, hunger, thirst, anger, joy, lust, pride, fear etc. The mind is the way in which we perceive the three different kinds of phenomena.

Over the past several centuries, much of the philosophical debate has been on the relationship between the brain and the mind. Brain is a physical object, and obeys laws of science. How then, can an abstract concept like mind trigger a physical response in this lump of grey matter, as happens when the mouth salivates at the sight of appetizing food?

The *Sankhya* and *Yoga* schools of Hindu philosophy, and Western Philosophers, Plato and Aristotle; and later in the 17th century, René Descartes advocated the theory of Dualism, in which mind (or soul) is considered to have existence independent of the brain (or the body).

Monism, on the other hand, is the position that mind and body are not ontologically different kinds of entities. Although there are Idealists (a section of monists) who believe that mind is all that exists, and the external world is an illusion created by the mind; the majority of monists maintain that only the entities postulated by physical theory exist, and that mind can be explained in terms of these entities. Most modern philosophers of mind adopt one of the many variants of this approach, maintaining in their different ways that the mind is not something separate from the body. These views have been particularly influenced by recent advances in the sciences, especially in the fields of sociobiology, computer science, evolutionary psychology and the various neurosciences.

Amygdala is an almond-shaped area of the brain that is responsible for the sense of fear. When an individual is frightened, the neurons in their amygdala are highly active. Clinical experiments have shown that mice, with amygdala surgically removed lose their fear for cats. This is an example of how a mental process like fear is related to a physical component of the brain. In the latter half of the 20th century we have learnt to actually 'see' thoughts play out in the brain on magnetic imaging devices which show activity in different areas of the brain. These are scientific evidences that consciousness resides in the brain.

Belief in dualism or monism is closely related to the belief in spirituality and faith, or in atheism and science. Consistent with the approach that I have taken in this book, I express my belief in monism over dualism. Mind is an expression of the brain. [16]

---

[16]   Triggered by accounts of Near Death Experiences, dualism has become a subject of considerable research by quantum scientists in the recent times. Relying on Heisenberg's Uncertainty Principle, they redefine 'soul' as quantum information residing in human brain cells, which is not destroyed upon the person's death, but is dissipated in the universe and can exist outside the body. This theory has been countered by neuroscientist Peter Clarke, who has evaluated the plausibility of these arguments based on quantum indeterminism, and has concluded that Heisenbergian uncertainty is too small to affect synaptic function. Besides, neural circuits have powerful noise-resistance mechanisms, which are more than sufficient to buffer against Heisenbergian effects. Other forms of quantum indeterminism could be considered, because these may be much greater than Heisenbergian uncertainty, but these have not so far been shown to play a role in the brain. This footnote is included only for the sake of completeness; the discussion of quantum souls will involve far too many scientific concepts to be within the scope of this book.

Mind and Computers

The conceptual difficulty in accepting the relationship between a concrete object, the brain, and an abstract mind could perhaps be eased if one takes the following example which is fundamental to computer science.

Consider a board with 4 light bulbs in a line, each connected to the power source through a separate switch. Suppose the first bulb from the right represents the value 1, the second 2, the third 4 and the fourth 8. (In other words, the value of the right-most bulb is 1; and of the other bulbs is twice the value of the bulb to its right). Switch on any of the bulbs arbitrarily. Let us suppose you have switched on the first and the third bulbs from the right. These bulbs represent 1 and 4 respectively. You can therefore say that the board, at this moment, represents 5 (=1+4). We will call this a *state* of the board. Now change the setting of the switches, and you will have a new state, representing a different value. You will find that this board is capable of 16 states, representing values from 0 (all bulbs switched off) to 15 (all bulbs switched on).

Now suppose we have added 2 bulbs to this board. The two newly added bulbs stand for 16 and 32. You can now have as many as 64 states on this board (representing values from 0 to 63). In general, with a board having **N** bulbs, you can get 2^N states.

As you can see, the number of states increases exponentially, as you increase the number of bulbs. With 15 bulbs, for example, you can get 2^{15} or 32,672 different states.

In this example, the hardware remains the same: a board with a certain number of bulbs. It is the numerous states that make the hardware represent numerous values.

A computer, with a memory of a few megabytes, is equivalent to a few million boards of 8 bulbs each. This can give you a very large number of combinations of a very large number of states. If each combination of states is displayed on the video monitor in a graphical form, there are an enormous number of graphical forms that can be represented on the monitor. And the computer, with the help of the program, can switch from one state to another very quickly. It is no wonder, therefore, that the relatively simple hardware of the computer can display an infinitely large number of graphical representations.

The human brain with billions of neurons can also have an astronomical number of combinations of a very large number of states. Each of these combinations represents a certain mental state. Just as the computer hardware is a physical entity, and obeys, for example, the law of gravitation; so does the brain. But just as a computer memory can store almost an infinite number of states, which can give an infinite variety to the output on the monitor, the brain can also have an infinite number of unique patterns, depending on the neurons that are fired; each representing a different mental process. Mental processes, though abstract in nature, reside in the brain, in the form of different states of the neurons, just as the software and other contents of the computer memory reside in the computer.

A computer program can pause for you to click with your mouse, and then, continue further depending on the input received from you. Here is a moment of interaction between the processes running inside the computer and a physical process (your finger pressing on the mouse button). In a similar fashion, mental processes can also interact with physical processes in both directions: mental processes can alter the physical processes, and *vice versa*. When you pass by a bakery, and air from the bakery brings the aroma of freshly baked cakes to your nostrils (physical process), you feel the urge to eat these cakes (mental process), and that urge forces you to go to the bakery (physical process again).

The Chemistry of Mind

More evidence of the interaction between the brain and the mind comes from the discovery of neuro-chemicals. Recent research has shown that these chemicals made in the brain cells are responsible for emotions in the mind. Scientists have identified a group of such chemicals inducing positive feelings like pleasure, happiness, romance and sexual arousal. Other emotions triggered by a combination of other neuro-chemicals include rage, fear, lust, panic and grief.

One important molecule is oxytocin, which was known for years as a trigger for child birth and lactation. Only recently was it found to induce a general happy and friendly feeling and to increase generosity, sharing, cooperation and trust. It is a hormone that is made in the brain, and is transported to, and secreted by, the pituitary gland, which is located at the base of the brain. It is released into defined regions of the brain that are involved in emotional, cognitive, and social behaviors. Hugging, cuddling or even shaking hands can induce a surge in oxytocin. Often referred to as the "love molecule", oxytocin is typically associated with helping couples establish a greater sense of intimacy and attachment.

Emotions, as we have seen earlier, are within the domain of the mind. But neuro-chemicals, produced in the brain

can induce and control emotions. Love is also Chemistry.
— And in more ways than one.

Conscience

Functioning and behavior of human mind have been studied by psychologists. Sigmund Freud and his followers see the mind as having three aspects, which work together to produce all of our complex behavior. They are the Id, the Ego and the Super Ego.

The Id functions in the irrational and emotional part of the mind. At birth a baby's mind is all Id – want, want and want. The Id is the primitive mind. It contains all the basic urges and feelings. It is the source for libido (psychic energy).

The Ego functions with the rational part of the mind. It is the 'front' to interact with society. The socialization of the individual involves the repression of natural, but antisocial desires. (We will talk more about these desires in Chapter 7). The Ego realizes the need for compromise and negotiates between the Id and the Super Ego. The Ego's job is to get the Id's pleasures but without offending the Super Ego.

The Super Ego is the moral part of the mind. It is an embodiment of parental and societal values. It stores and enforces rules and restricts the instinctive behavior of the individual. Its power to enforce rules comes from its ability to create anxiety, shame and guilt.

The Super Ego divides into two activities: Ego Ideal and Conscience. Freud based this idea on the way that parents behave towards their children as they bring them up. The Ego Ideal provides rules for good behavior, and standards of excellence towards which the Ego must strive. The Ego ideal is basically what the child's parents approve of or value. The child expects that the parents will reward 'good' behavior with praise. It learns to appreciate the parents' approval and feels pride in satisfying their expectations. The Conscience holds the rules about what constitutes bad behavior. The Conscience is basically all those things that the child feels the parents will disapprove of or punish. The child feels guilt and shame at letting its parents down. These feelings of shame and guilt become established in the psyche as the conscience.

Life and Death

Life is chemistry, and consciousness is electro-chemistry. Consciousness holds an individual's identity – everything that is private to the individual, accessible only to that person, and to nobody else. It has memories and experiences, pleasant and not so pleasant; all learnings; beliefs and convictions; emotions – love[17], hatred, fear, aspirations, jealousy; aptitudes, talents and hobbies; nature and habits; and much more that makes a person so uniquely what he is.

When vital organs of the body fail, either due to natural or other reasons, the person drifts towards death. Failure of body systems spreads, and if this is not arrested and corrected in time, eventually the heart is not able to cope with the requirements, and stops pumping. When oxygen is not supplied, all organs, including the brain die. Clinically, death is defined as an absence of brain activity as measured by EEG.

---

[17]   Contrary to the romantic notion that love is a matter of heart and not of mind, the only role that the heart plays is to pump more blood to the brain, where the excitement among neurons results in a higher demand for oxygen

When the brain dies, so do the individual neurons in the brain, and the state which they represented just before the death. It is like switching off the power supply to a computer: the memory is wiped out; and all software and information that is stored in the memory is also lost for ever. (The computer can be switched on again when the power is restored, and the memory can be loaded with its original contents. This is where brains are different from computers). With the death of the body, the mind, the conscious self, the soul also dies.

The most striking features of death are its permanency and irreversibility. The permanent stoppage of all mental processes and erasure of the person's perceptions take away from him everything that gave that person the unique identity. He has no emotions for people who were once dear to him. Gone also is the pain and the fear he may have had. If he was a musician, he has now lost his innate ability to create music in his mind, and reproduce it. If he was an author, he will never generate any fresh ideas, and express them.

All that remains of him is memories. Hard copies of memories like photographs and letters — and for some, recordings of their music, paintings, books or essays — are theoretically permanent, but in practice, they will last as long as they are relevant. Soft copies are memories stored in the minds of people who may have interacted with him, and cannot outlast those minds.

When a person dies, his body is interred, cremated or disposed of in some other way. Over a period of time, (immediately in case of cremation), the molecules of his body, and the atoms from these molecules mix with nature – soil, air and water. Matter is indestructible, and these atoms will remain forever, and may find their way into another living organism, through the air that it breathes, the food it eats and the water it takes. Atoms in your body may also have belonged to other humans, animals or any other organisms in the past. But this recycling of atoms is not reincarnation, because firstly, not all atoms of the original body would have ended up in the same new body; and secondly, these atoms do not have memory – they cannot give any clue of where they were before they entered the present body. And not even a trace of the *mind* or the *consciousness* of the previous owner is carried along with the atoms.

A dualist maintains that soul is immortal, and leaves the body upon its death. The soul remains suspended, (and sometimes manifests itself as a ghost or a spirit), until it enters an unborn body, and begins another life on Earth. To a monist, the soul is an integral part of the human body, resides in the brain and is manifested by the numerous states of the neurons. The soul dies with the body, and is lost for ever. Not being matter, the soul is not conserved, and certainly plays no part in the formation of a new life: A fertilized egg is all that is required to create a new life.

And this is no longer in the realm of hypotheses and arguments. In the recent years, scientists have successfully 'created' life in laboratories by fertilizing an egg with a sperm.

And the recipe has not mentioned adding a dash of soul.

6

FATE

Even people, who claim everything is predestined,
look before they cross the road

-Stephen Hawking

A young man crosses a street. A car is speeding towards him, and passes the spot that the man had passed only a fraction of a second later. The man successfully crosses the road, does many things over the next few hours, days and years, meets a young woman **A**, and marries her, and has two children: **B** and **C**. They have a long married life, during which, he meets many people and interacts with their lives before he dies many years later. The motorist, after passing the young man, goes to where he was going, spends his day as he had planned; and no one thinks about the other possibility: What would have happened if the pedestrian had been one step slower, or the car a few feet faster. Things would have been very different. The fatal accident would have terminated the life of the pedestrian, plunged his friends and family into grief, which would have lasted, perhaps for some of them, for the rest of their lives. The motorist would also not be able to spend the rest of the day as he had earlier planned, and the shadow of the accident would hang over his life for ever. The young woman, **A**, happily unaware that the person involved in that fatal accident was to be her future husband, would marry another man and have two children: **X** and **Y**.

What we are looking at are two alternative scenarios: the first as things actually panned out, and the second, the way they would have, if one step had been taken differently. There are a lot of happy people in the first scenario; and many more whose lives have been affected to some degree by future interactions with the young man. The girl, **A**, is certainly one of them, since her life in the two scenarios would be very different. Children **B** and **C**; and their children and grandchildren would be absent in the second scenario, just as **X** and **Y** and their descendants in the first. Life would be very different for a lot of people, because of that one step.

Billions of people in the world constantly do things that affect the future for themselves and for many other people, and they are all one step away from changing the future of all these people. There are multiple future scenarios created every moment involving a lot of people. If we aggregate all these scenarios, we will end up with infinite possible scenarios for the future.[18]

But only one of those scenarios is actually going to play out.

---

[18] Conceptually, imagine a node (an action point), and several branches (alternative possible outcomes) emerging from it. Each branch, in turn, after a short distance, has another node with more branches, and so on, resulting in a tree-like structure. This will be referred to as the Scenario-Tree in this book. A possible scenario is a continuous line passing through some of the nodes, and running along some of the branches.

Is the one scenario that will eventually play out pre-determined? Is this selection inviolable? Is it possible to know in advance what this scenario is? Theories of Fate examine these questions.

Theories of Fate

There are three different theories relating to Fate. The Strong Fatalistic Theory (SFT) believes that the one scenario that plays out has been determined beforehand, and is known to us only as events unfold. This scenario is what we call Fate, and no matter what we do, we cannot win against Fate. Those who believe in SFT have to accept that every step that they take has been predetermined, and they cannot, by their own volition, change anything. The pedestrian, in our example, could not have taken a different step (and met with a fatal accident), because doing so would have changed the fate of several people, including some from a future generation, which, SFT believes has been pre-decided. A line from an Indian folksong describes the futility of human effort in a universe pre-determined by Fate: 'If you believe that you are doing anything of your volition, you are as naive as a dog, running beneath a cart, and thinking that he is carrying the load of the cart.'

The mystique of SFT seems to have lured people to use this in many mythological and fantasy stories, but the futility of human effort against a pre-determined outcome over which man has no control has tended to make believers in SFT complacent. Why should we study for the exams, if the result is pre-determined? And why invoke the Personal God, by praying before a job interview if the outcome is pre-determined and inviolable? (But then again, our act of studying / not studying or praying / not praying is also pre-determined, and is not left to our choice).

SFT raises questions similar to the ones we have dealt with before: Who has decided the fate, and when? As to the first question, the only possibility that comes to mind is God. (Not again! Not another responsibility for Him!). Having argued against God's role in the creation of universe, administration of it, creation of life and the continuing evolution, it is difficult to accept Him in yet another role, just because He is disguised, this time, as Fate.

As to when fate was determined, if the scenario that is playing out has been scripted in advance, the role played by each entity in the scene must have been decided *at the same time* in the past. The precision required in the interaction between entities would not be possible otherwise. (A fraction of a second, as we saw in the example above, stood between two different scenarios). And since the chain of events comprising the scenario goes back to the beginning of life on Earth, it would be fair to expect that that is when the one scenario to be played out must have been decided.[19] If the story in the scenario selected includes a situation in which Man meets an extra-terrestrial at some future time, the fate must have been decided before any life was created in the universe; and we may safely put the date as when the universe was created.

---

[19]   Fate need not be limited to living beings only. Inanimate objects may also play a role in the story as it unfolds. For example if the pedestrian in the example above, had tripped over a stone lying on the road, the outcome could have been affected. Thus positions and movements of *all* objects – animate and inanimate; and for all times, should have been determined at the same time.

More questions need to be answered, like where in this universe is the chosen scenario 'stored' in a codified form, and how does He ensure that events that take place are in conformity with this scenario at all times? Why, with so much intelligence having evolved on Earth is nobody able to break the code and decipher the scenario that will play out in the future? There are people who have made a claim to have acquired that knowledge, but all such claims have been proven wrong. (Once again, if the scenario does not include a player who successfully deciphers the code, the code will always remain a mystery).

The second theory is the Weak Fatalistic Theory (WFT), which is SFT, but compromised for convenience. WFT believes that Fate is not cast in stone, and can be altered, from time to time, through human effort and by God's grace (or wrath). The believers of Fate may have considered this compromise necessary, because SFT lulls people to complacency and reduces the role of Personal God. In this weaker version, SFT has been relaxed in several ways. First, the fate is supposed to have been determined, not for all living beings in the universe in the beginning, but for each (human) individual at the time of birth[20]. This weakens the logic of fatality, because determining the fate of one individual in isolation, independent of the fate of other individuals, who are already born, or are yet to be born, and with whom this person will interact, would result in many clashes and contradictions. For example, when the fate of a male child, **X**, is written at the time of his birth, would it

---

[20] According to a Hindu belief, the God of Fate writes the fate for a child when it is 5 days old. What the infant does in the first 5 days, without a blueprint is, according to the ardent believers of Fate, unimportant.

be known at that time who his wife would be (presumably younger, and not yet born)? And when and where they would marry? If so, would it be a part of her parents' fate to engage in a conjugal activity on a particular date, so that a girl child is produced to suit the fate of **X**? And would the writer of fate 'remember' to write in her fate, that she is meant to marry **X** at the same time and place? If the answers to all these questions are in the affirmative, there is hardly any difference between this variety of WFT and SFT.

Another flexibility allowed in WFT is with regard to the timing of an event. For example, you may be told by someone professing to be able to read your future, that you *may* get a promotion at the age of 28; but if not, there is another chance at the age of 32. This flexibility in timing clearly goes against the logic of fate. Recall the pedestrian-motorist example where only a fraction of a second stood between two very different scenarios. Or take another example: Two persons stand one behind the other in a queue to buy a lottery ticket. The first ticket wins the jackpot, the other nothing. Again a small difference in time results in a large difference in fortune. The ambiguity in the time in the prediction of promotion was, presumably, introduced to remove the complacency that an absolute prediction may cause. Now you are told that conditions will be favorable for a promotion during certain periods, but you will have to work hard to grab the chance; but that leaves WFT logically unexplainable.

WFT leaves adequate room for a Personal God. Since flexibility in how the future unfolds is allowed in WFT, (and endeavor alone does not always produce the desired result), a person may pray to God before an examination or a job interview requesting a divine intervention to see him through. If he is fated to clear the exam or get the job, God need only file his prayers. Otherwise, through his prayers, he is asking God to *switch from one scenario to another*, in which he has a successful resolution to his immediate problem. (Never mind if the new scenario dashes the aspirations of a whole lot of other persons). Of course, God will keep receiving many such prayers from the earthlings, and in a small fraction of cases, He would, according to WFT, grant the wishes out of turn. This would require constant switching of scenarios, and at the same time keeping track to ensure that there are no unintended changes because of the constant switches. Is this possible to do, especially when there are infinite possible alternative scenarios? For God, it is – he is omnipotent. But why do we need to invent a theory that places so much burden on God, who we had said need not exist in order to explain the universe and our lives in it?

The questions about where the individual's fate is stored in a codified form and how this code is administered remain to be answered. Pseudo-Scientific explanations, linking the fate of an individual to planetary positions at the time of his / her birth, and its administration to planetary movements have no real scientific basis. The only way planetary bodies are known to affect another body like Earth is through the force of gravitation; and that force cannot even begin to explain marriages, promotions and other events in the lives of people on Earth.

Sitting opposite SFT in the spectrum of theories of Fate is the Non-Fatalistic Theory (NFT). This theory believes that no event is pre-determined; that events just *happen*. And the future is flexible enough to take its course, based on the events that have occurred. If SFT is like a tightly scripted play, where every actor speaks or moves only according to the script, NFT is a play without a script, or even a story, where each actor is allowed to ad lib, and the story moves forward depending on the earlier acts of each actor[21]. The questions that we have discussed in the context of the earlier two theories clearly do not apply to NFT. Nor are there any logical inconsistencies that need explanation.

Is there a scope for human endeavor in NFT? Of course, there is. Since the future scenario is neither pre-decided nor inviolable, any human action is allowed to alter the scenario. With every act of yours, you choose one among the many branches of the Scenario-Tree and close the others. But where that branch will eventually lead you will depend not only on your further action, but also the acts of many others that affect that branch of the Scenario-Tree. Your act alone does not determine the end result.

In order to choose from among the three theories of Fate, a principle known as Occam's Razor, may be helpful. Occam's Razor is a logical principle enunciated in the 14th century, which states that one should not make more assumptions than the minimum needed. When faced with competing hypotheses, the simplest explanation requiring the fewest assumptions is more likely to be accurate than more complicated explanations involving too many assumptions. Occam's Razor has found applications in fields as diverse as Science, philosophy, religion and the probability theory.

---

[21]   Taking this analogy forward, WFT is like a soap-opera running for 10 years or more, switching its storyline at the audience's request and director's whims; and with no end objective in mind.

If one applies the Occam's Razor to the theories of fate, it is evident that NFT, with virtually no assumptions required, passes the test. Both other theories that assume pre-ordained future need to make a number of assumptions to explain the way fate is pre-determined and how it plays out, requiring even more assumptions to answer questions arising from these explanations[22].

Yet, most of us come from a paradigm, where accepting NFT may not be easy. I will try to foresee some of the objections, and to dispel them by encouraging a change of paradigm.

Divine Conspiracy

A businessman, **M**, has booked himself on an evening flight to another city, where he has to attend a meeting the next day. The meeting is so important, that his absence is sure to mean loss of a large business deal. He therefore leaves his office that afternoon, early enough to be able to reach the airport on time. Unfortunately for him, riots have broken out in the city, and the police have closed many roads, including an arterial road to the airport. **M** asks his driver to take side-roads, but they are jammed with traffic. Fretting and fuming, when **M** finally reaches the airport, he is informed that his flight has just left. There is no other flight that evening; the first flight the next day reaches too late for him to attend the meeting, and that flight is also full. Dejected, he returns home, knowing that he has lost the

---

[22] The reader will notice that our rejection of God in the different roles discussed in the earlier chapters, as well as the discussion on religion in the next chapter also satisfy the Occam test, as explanations justifying the contrary are always long-winded and require several assumptions.

business deal, cursing the traffic and the riots. On reaching home, he switches on the TV, and finds that the flight that he had missed has crashed within minutes of the take off, and all passengers on board have died.

Another person, whose office was closer to the airport also wanted to go to the same destination for work that was important to him; but having booked late, he was wait-listed on the same flight. He had very little hope of getting a booking when he went to the airport; and was pleasantly surprised, when 15 minutes before the scheduled take-off, he was told that there was a 'no show', and he can now board the flight. He had just enough time to call his wife, **N**, to tell her that he was flying, after all.

Both **M** and **N** now have reasons to believe in Fate. **M** believes that he was destined to survive, and destiny had ensured that he was held up in traffic long enough to miss the ill-fated flight. **N** also believes that it was in her husband's destiny to die a violent death. Why, otherwise, would a passenger with a confirmed ticket cancel his booking at the eleventh hour? (It was a No Show, and not cancellation; but **N** does not know that).

An emotionally moving experience like this may result in irrational thinking for both **M** and **N**. But if they later analyzed the events rationally, this is what they would realize. In their way of thinking, the destiny had become the cause, and what led to the destiny had become the effect. *Because* **M** had to survive, the riots had occurred. *Because* **N**'s husband had to die, someone cancelled his booking. Both clauses starting with '*Because*' are causes, and the riots and cancellation have become effects. There is one problem here: Causes always precede Effects. **M**'s survival cannot be seen as a cause for the riots, because riots have happened earlier. Similarly, the death of **N**'s husband cannot be the reason for the cancellation, which happened earlier.

The correct way of looking at this incident is to move in the forward direction:

M: Riots → Traffic → Missed the flight → Survived
N's husband: Cancellation by a passenger
→ Confirmed booking → Death

It is a lot easier (and the correct way) to place the cause first and then the effect. If you want to inquire into the reason for riots, look *backwards*. Perhaps a local leader was assaulted. But don't look for an event in future as the cause for the riots, like the survival of **M**. Similarly, why did the plane crash? Not to kill **N**'s husband. But because of an engine trouble.

There is a tendency on the part of many people to believe that whatever is happening to them is a part of a divine design, and it is to facilitate this, that many things have happened earlier. But this is a self-centered view. For example, what about the other 300 people who died in the plane crash? Fate would have to be an incredible conspirator to have assembled 300 people who 'had to die'; weeded out the one person, who 'had to survive', created riots to facilitate his survival, (never mind the effect that these riots would have had on the lives of the other people in the city), and pushed in one more person, who also 'had to die', whom Fate had arranged to be placed at the top of the waiting-list! Instead of seeing life as a complex divine conspiracy, isn't it much more rational to follow the cause and effect chain to explain what has happened?

Do not look for an ulterior motive to justify events. They are not based on anything other than past events that have mechanically caused them.

Born with a Silver Spoon

A school boy, **J,** from a family of modest means has, for a classmate, **K**, the son of a rich industrialist. Although **J** realizes that **K** is more privileged — has a car to drop him and pick him up from school, hosts the best birthday parties among all the classmates, etc.; he is too young to think about the 'injustice' that nature has meted out to him. But when the two have grown together, and **J,** academically brighter of the two, sees that he has to struggle to find a decent job, while **K** has a bright future waiting for him to step into, he may ask himself, why there should be so much difference between their lives. The answer, obviously, is that he is born to middle-class parents, and **K** is born to a rich industrialist; and without any grievance against his caring parents, **J** is forced to ask: Why are the hardships of a middle-class family written in *my* fate? What has **K** done to deserve being born in a rich family? *Why wasn't I born to richer parents?*

This is an illogical question. If you were not born to the parents you were born to, you would not be the person you are.

Once again, the cause-effect relationship will allow us to analyze the situation correctly. The conjugal act of a couple is the cause, and the child is its effect. If a middle-class couple performs the conjugal act that produces the child **J**, he is born to middle-class parents; and if a rich couple produces a child **K**, he is born to rich parents. In the question: 'Why wasn't *I* born to richer parents?', the identity of '*I*' is established only after the irreversible act of being born, and hence the question is meaningless. If **J** is asking such a question, he is perhaps motivated by the theory that he existed before the conjugal act of his parents, (in the form of a floating soul), and Fate allotted middle-class parents to him, instead of a pair of richer parents. But since we have seen no need to assume portability of souls, as discussed in the last chapter, it does not make sense to ask: 'Why I am born to the parents I am born to'.[23]

Why am I here?

Many of us have asked this question to ourselves at least once: Why have I come on this Earth? Some of us have spent a life time mulling this question over.

The only answer is: Because your parents had engaged in a conjugal activity nine months earlier. After this, the laws of bio-chemistry took over, and resulted in you. You will remain on Earth as long as the bio-chemical systems of your body allow, and when they don't, (sometimes triggered by an accident or other forms of violence), you will die.

Spiritual thinkers may find this answer very flippant; as they believe that there is a purpose for which they have been given a return ticket to this planet — like knowing God,

---

[23] However, it is logical for parents to ask: "why is our child the way it is", because the parents have caused the child to be born, and have also developed its faculties to make what he/she is. It is sensible to ask this question, because here, unlike in the earlier one, the cause precedes the effect.

becoming enlightened, cleansing the soul, doing selfless service, or helping others; but they are once again making the mistake of imputing a divine purpose for everything that happens. People spend an enormous part of their lives trying to discover this divine mission, and even if they think they have found it, there may be very little life left to do anything about it. If there really was a divine purpose, why didn't the divinity let you know about it on your eighteenth birthday? Or tell your parents about it on your fifth birthday? You could then have guided the rest of your life better. But, according to spiritual thinkers, discovering the answer to this question is itself a part of the mission in one's life.

We may say that Mahatma Gandhi, Martin Luther King Jr. and Nelson Mandela had a mission in their lives: to work for socio-political justice for those discriminated against. But were they *fated* to work on this mission? Was it a divine mission that they were sent to Earth with? Or did they *choose* their mission, based on their conviction, their character and the circumstances around them? To believe that fate sent them to Earth with a mission to set India free from the colonial powers; or to eradicate racism from USA and apartheid from South Africa would be like putting the cart before the horse.

Make Your Own Destiny

All of us have experienced that our efforts to achieve a task do not always bear fruit. Those who believe that fate is pre-ordained and nothing can change what is written in their fate are likely to give up trying, and will learn to accept whatever fate decides for them.

As we have seen, future events are not pre-decided. They happen on the basis of actions being taken now: by you *and* by others. If your action does not yield the expected result, very likely, it is because of an action by someone else. That person may not even know you, or have any intention of foiling your attempts; but his action affects the branch of the Scenario-Tree that you had chosen earlier, and takes you away from your goal. Those who, in the wake of failures, get disheartened, blame their destiny and stop trying would not attain their goals. They would be like rudderless boats in a stream, drifting with the current, and going wherever it takes them. To reach even close to the desired goal, you must try to steer the boat in that direction, in spite of events not under your control. *Bhagvad Gita* has underscored the importance of action (*karma*) versus passivity. Remember that there is no divine conspiracy which is determined to foil every effort you make. You have a better chance of success if you kept trying, instead of leaving your life in the hands of an unknown fate.

In the words of Swami Vivekananda:

> We reap what we sow. We are the makers of our own fate. The wind is blowing; those vessels whose sails are unfurled catch it, and go forward on their way, but those which have their sails furled do not catch the wind. Is that the fault of the wind... We make our own destiny.

If belief in SFT results in complacency, NFT encourages action.

7

NEED FOR RELIGION

I do not believe in God. But I do fear Him.

- Anonymous

A few years ago, I watched an exciting TV series, where a plane crashes on an uninhabited island, and leaves a few survivors. There is no hope that there would be a rescue mission, and they realize that they will have to stay on this island for a long, long time; and have for company for the rest of their lives, people who were strangers just a few hours ago. They face the same problems that the early man may have faced: Food, Shelter and Security – security from predators on the island, and security from their companions. They also realize that the laws, ethics and etiquette that they had been following before they were marooned on this island no longer applied; and they had a unique opportunity to create their own rules for their society. The early episodes of the serial showed how, even when handed a clean slate, they end up devising rules very similar to those that exist in the world outside. In their little society, as in our civilization, 'each man for himself' was not a viable approach; friendship and love grew among strangers;

and help, care and sacrifice brought people together to form a strong group with common objectives. Of course, mystery and excitement are more important for the Television Rating Points of a serial than lessons in Civics; so after the first few episodes, the show raced off in a different direction.

Social Norms and Religion

Man, by nature, has certain basic instincts, which are anarchic. For the preservation of civilization, such impulses must be kept under check. Sexual lust, for example, is a strong impulse. If a man had his way, he would 'steal' all women that he would like to be with. If such an impulse were allowed unchecked, the institution of family would not survive. People want to possess things that they like, even if they belong to somebody else. Taking them by force or by deceit is also a natural impulse; but if society turned a blind eye to this, no one in the society would feel safe possessing anything. Violence, as an outlet for anger is another destructive impulse which can lead to large scale destruction of property and lives. Society must moderate this reaction, so that people can live in society without fear.

Society has therefore evolved codes of conduct, norms, morals and rules, whose objective is to preserve the civilization, to prevent it from sliding back to the primeval society; and to create an atmosphere where all members of the society can contribute to the attainment of their shared objectives. Civilization is the thin veneer that covers the basic, destructive instincts, which lurk below the surface and constantly threaten to burst out.

All social rules necessarily go to restrain these basic impulses. Laws ask us not to steal, rape or cause violence.

No laws are required in the context of impulses which are beneficial to the society – such as the urge to make somebody happy or to protect one's family. Hence every law, every rule made by society seeks to curb some of the destructive instincts innate in a man and requires effort on the part of the man to stay within this rule.

To ensure that all individuals within the society obey these rules, society has created institutions for justice and law enforcement. But not all transgressions of societal rules are noticed, or can be punished. The society has to find means other than the judicial and law enforcement institutions that it has created.

There are two other courts that exist, or have been devised, outside the formal institutions for justice. The first of these uses the individual's conscience. As we have seen earlier, conscience originates in the Super Ego, and takes its cue from one's parents during childhood. But as the child grows, other influences and experiences shape the ethical values and the conscience of the individual. The consequence of not obeying one's conscience is 'guilt', which leaves a scar that may keep bothering the individual. Conscience is thus a societal construct which checks the person who is on the verge of doing something 'wrong', and if he disobeys the call of his conscience, the guilty feeling that he develops is his punishment. The efficacy of this court of justice depends on how strong one's conscience is, and which acts are considered as transgressions. Each society has moral standards, which define the acts which are considered acceptable and those which are not. Society drills these moral codes at every stage in the life of its members. As to the strength of the conscience, it is up to the individual to use self-discipline and build a strong and discerning conscience.

The second court of justice that the society leans on is religion and God. American psychologist Matt Rossano contends that when humans began living in larger groups, they may have *created* gods as a means of enforcing morality. In small groups, morality can be enforced by social forces such as gossip or reputation. However it is much harder to enforce morality using social forces in much larger groups. He indicates that by including ever watchful gods and spirits, humans discovered an effective strategy for restraining selfishness and building more cooperative groups.

Along with religion come the belief in supernatural power and the threat that those who break the moral codes will be punished by this super power[24]. Virtually all the concepts that we saw, and dismissed in the earlier chapters as being irrational, form the basis for the religious belief system. But in spite of the irrationality, religion plays a vital role in the society, for it inculcates the belief in people that they would be punished or rewarded by God for their behavior. It is difficult to educate the masses about the niceties of civics. It is a lot easier to create a myriad of mythological stories, illustrating the concepts and the morals. Readers will be able to see how the misconceptions that we have dealt with so far have entered the belief systems of the people in the name of religion.

Different societies have evolved differently, and so have different religions. Hence it is difficult to list comprehensively, all religious misconceptions. What follows is a sample of such religious beliefs. However, it must be borne in mind that the intention in popularizing these

---

[24]   Although belief in God is the hallmark of religion, there are exceptions, like Buddhism, where spiritual beings have only minor importance

beliefs is noble – to ensure that the masses follow the norms which are necessary to protect our civilization and control their destructive instincts.

The Super Power

God is believed to be omnipresent – He is everywhere. You have nowhere to hide. Even if you commit your evil deed in the farthest and darkest corner of Earth, God is there to watch you. He is omniscient. He knows everything: He even knows your thoughts, so keep your thoughts clean. Also if he has agreed to answer your prayers before an examination, you can depend on God to know the intricate details of the subject – whether it is Calculus or Company Law. And God is omnipotent. He can achieve anything – either when he decides to help you or to teach you a lesson.

Rational thinkers have found that the qualities of omnipresence, omniscience and omnipotence are mutually contradictory. For example, consider the logical absurdity in the idea of omnipotence: Can God create a rock which He Himself cannot lift? Yes or no, there is something He cannot achieve.

But leave logic to the skeptics: Religion is about blind faith.

Personal God

Most believers talk to God, either in their minds or aloud. Sometimes they say 'Sorry', sometimes 'Thank you'; but most often, 'Please'. The omniscient God knows, for each devotee, all their misdeeds to match the 'sorry' with; and prayers that are granted to account for the 'thank you'. And the Omnipotent God has to be pleased by offering prayers (and sometimes bribe), if the devotee wants something done, no matter how impossible it may be. Why God, who has already shouldered so many responsibilities, should take on this massive additional responsibility, is not known; but *how* he would carry out this responsibility is not in question: He is a Super Power. Incidentally, animals are not known to pray. Why is God partial to the human species?

There may also be questions regarding why God may grant favors requested by one devotee, and not another, if their requests are mutually exclusive. If one devotee prays to God before an examination that the questions be from the limited portion of the syllabus that he has studied, why should God listen to his prayers and not of another person, who has skipped this particular portion, and has concentrated on another portion? Or if a devotee prays before a job interview that he be selected for the one opening out of the fifty candidates, why should God grant his wishes and not of another applicant for the same position? Religion has a theory for how God's mind works in such situations; and it is the subject matter of Divine Justice.

Divine Justice

In the physical world, we constantly see cause-effect relationships. You press a switch, and a bulb lights up. You turn a key in the car ignition, and the engine roars to life. You provide an input, and you receive an output. In the world of human experiences also, religion makes us believe, such relationships exist. You give alms to a waif, and an ailing member of your family feels relief. Again, logic and scientific reasoning are thrown out of the window. There is an electrical wire connecting the switch and the bulb; and there is a lot of other hardware that makes the seemingly simple cause-effect relationship work. The same applies to the car. But there is no such relationship between the act of charity and the health of your family member. We accept the principle of 'do good and good will happen to you' easily, because religion explains it to us by giving examples from the physical world that we are familiar with.

But there are two problems with such simplistic explanations. What is a *good* deed, what is a *bad* deed? There is no absolute definition – different societies have different views at different times. For example, pre-marital sex is considered a grave sin in certain societies; but other societies have accepted it. Similarly, what is a good outcome and what is a bad outcome? Death of a family member is a very sad event, but in some families, the inheritance that results from the death can be a cause for celebration.

Another analogy which is a favorite with religious teachers is: A good act is like a bank deposit: it increases the bank balance. A bad act reduces the balance. The benefit that you can reap in your life is proportional to the bank balance. Nice lesson; explained with the help of a real-life example: but who is to audit your account to make sure that you reaped the right amount of benefit?

For the masses, such a doctrine of Divine Justice is very useful, because though devoid of logic, this carrot-and-stick approach works. Fear of divine retribution may induce a man to suppress an urge to do something immoral, even if no one else is likely to know about his misdeed. But how do you answer a person who points out that he has sacrificed many opportunities to make money dishonestly, and yet has never enjoyed happiness; and his neighbor, who is a crook, lives like a king? This is when you tell him that this birth is not the only birth: there were many births earlier, and there will be many more to come.

And the bank balance will be carried forward to the next birth.

Cycle of Rebirth

As I have mentioned before, different religions developed differently, and not all religions have the same belief systems. Rebirth is one such concept, which while very strong in some religions, is rejected by others.

Belief in rebirth is related to the belief in the duality of body and soul. Religions that subscribe to this duality, believe that the soul, once out of the body floats around, till it is assigned to another body, (not necessarily human). The state at which the person is reborn (rich *vs.* poor family; good & caring *vs.* indifferent parents) is decided by the *karmic* balance in the account of the soul. During the course of each worldly life, actions committed (good or evil) determine the future destiny of each being. This process goes on until the person achieves *Moksha*, the freedom from the cycle of rebirth.

Belief in the rebirth cycle has some romantic connotations also, which are not strictly religious. Unfulfilled love, according to this belief, can be consummated in the next birth – a fantasy which has found favor in mythology and romantic tales. Belief in the duality of body and soul also leads to the imagination that souls which have left one body but have not found another, are hanging around, and may haunt those associated with the most recent incarnation as ghosts and spirits.

Fate

Many theologies, ambiguously, believe that fate is determined by God, but He reserves the right to intervene and change the fate. We saw the incompatibility of these two thoughts in the last chapter; but religion maintains the ambiguity because, on the one hand, man cannot afford to be complacent, while on the other, he sometimes needs the comfort of believing that his honest efforts failed, because 'fate had chosen otherwise'.

Belief in fate also promotes optimism in man. The basic principle of fate: 'Everything happens for a reason' is slightly modified to 'Everything happens for a *good* reason' to soften the blow of failure. If a man does not get a job that he had applied for, it is because fate has planned a better job for him, which the man would not have got if he had taken the first job. Father Fate keeps track of all the seven billion earthlings, and plans the best for each one of them. And what happens if you don't get a better job in the second and the third attempt also? Life is long, and you should keep your faith in fate. And then there is always the next life.

It is obvious that rational thinking has no place in religion. In fact, religion prescribes that one must have *blind faith* in divinity. And patience. You score minus points, if you raise doubts. And yet, religion has a very important role to play in keeping the society together. It is possible to imagine a world without God; but not without religion.[25]

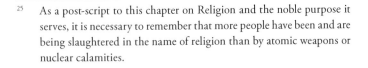

---

[25] As a post-script to this chapter on Religion and the noble purpose it serves, it is necessary to remember that more people have been and are being slaughtered in the name of religion than by atomic weapons or nuclear calamities.

98

8

BEYOND GOD

The only tyrant I accept in this world is the still voice within

- Mahatma Gandhi

So far we have seen a very gloomy picture of the universe. God does not exist. The universe was self-created by an accident and is self-administered. Life was also created by an accident, and has been evolving on its own. We come from nothing and return to nothing, never to come back on Earth again. There is no perpetuity of soul, no past or future births, and no *Moksha* or salvation for the soul. No divine justice that punishes the bad deeds or rewards the good ones. No purpose or a divine mission for our journey to the Earth. Please, *pleeease* let there be an argument that proves that all this is not true. Let us return to our secure belief that there is God up above, and He will take care of His children.

Even those who consider themselves atheists often echo this sentiment. Belief in God is a psychological and emotional need. Just as we need a mentor, a big brother or a father figure to guide us when we are in doubt, to offer us a big shoulder to cry on, to listen patiently to our confession when we have done something wrong; we need God, *even if we know that he does not exist.* He is like the imaginary friend that some children (and sometimes adults) talk to, whom only they can see and hear. A prop that provides the psychological comfort that the disturbed person may require.

Has rationality arising out of scientific thinking taken away from us something that we desperately need for our psychological and emotional well being? Can we substitute it with something else, without submitting to the irrationality of pretending to believe in what we know cannot be true? In this last part of this book, I would like to discuss my thoughts on what we should pin our beliefs on.

Life Mission

Rationality tells us that we have not come here with a divine mission. But that need not mean that we should not carve out a mission in our lives, and try sincerely to accomplish it. We have talked, in earlier chapters, about Gandhi, King and Mandela; and their missions. They were leaders with large following and their missions had far-reaching effects. We may not all be leaders, and our mission may not be adopted by others. Of course, it would be creditable if we embarked on a noble mission that many others could follow; but even if we did not, a personal mission that helps us plan our lives, and guides us whenever we are at crossroads is important to have. Indeed, without such a mission, life will drift till the inevitable end.

But what is wrong with that? We did not *plan* to be on this Earth. Why should we carry any responsibility? Who do we owe this responsibility to?

I have two suggestions.

Life is Beautiful

Our life span on this Earth is very short. If you consider the age of the universe, and assume that it will continue for the same period of time in the future, and plot this time line along the equator of the Earth, our life span would be an insignificantly small line of ten centimeters. Out of eternity, this is the only time allotted to our life.

And once we leave this Earth, we are never going to return.

Think now, of the improbability of our getting a life at all. A man has 23 pairs of chromosomes, and during meiosis, one chromosome, at random, from each of the 23 pairs is selected to represent him in the germ cell (sperm). He can therefore produce 2^{23} different sperms. Similarly, the egg that a woman produces each month is one of the 2^{23} different eggs that she can produce. There are, therefore, $2^{23} \times 2^{23}$ or 70 trillion unique fertilized eggs, that a couple can produce. Each fertilized egg represents a life – a unique human being. Every one of us on this Earth has had to fight extremely heavy odds, to be given a life on Earth, in preference to 70 trillion other possible siblings.

If you consider these facts and figures, you do not need God to tell you what your mission should be: Make most of your life. It is a gift that chance has given you by depriving trillions of others. You will have a very brief time on this Earth; so make every moment count, no matter how life treats you. Don't waste these precious moments asking why others have been given a better deal. Be happy in your life. You will not get another chance to live your life.

This philosophy is aptly expressed in this couplet:

The unborn tomorrow, the dead yesterday
Why fret about them if today be sweet!

There can be no single definition of happiness in life, and no single formula to achieve it. But the following comments can apply in most cases.

A happy life needs physical and mental well being and strength. *Yoga* is a school of Hinduism and some other Eastern philosophies which prescribes physical exercises, controlled breathing exercises and dietary regulations for physical wellness, and deep concentration and meditation to sharpen the memory, strengthen will power and provide mental strength. Equally important is the emotional strength. Since everyone is bound to face moments of sorrow, fear and other unhappy emotions in their lives, it is necessary to be emotionally stable. This requires conscious training, and the goal is to prevent the mind from feeling extreme emotions – either of exultation or of misery.

Several articles and books have been written which, without relying on a specific religion, discuss the philosophy of happiness, and suggest how to attain it in life. Even an extract from such articles could provide enough material for a series of books. I am not going to attempt that here, but I will close this discussion by making an important point.

Your mission to achieve happiness in life cannot be fulfilled without having your conscience on your side. According to Sigmund Freud, guilt is the tension that occurs between the individual desires that stem from the ego and the values held in the super ego. When people consciously make a choice that violates the moral codes which they are committed to, it leaves a painful scar on their conscience. One of the greatest psychological and emotional needs of an individual is to have a clear conscience.

Preserve Civilization

We know that an orderly universe, with our Earth in it, has come about as the result of a very rare accident. Life on Earth was another accident. It has taken billions of years of natural selection to evolve the primitive life into an intelligent, human life. It took millennia of social evolution for civilization to reach where it is today. It stands on culture, ethics, values and morals, which have kept adapting with time. It derives strength from the scientific and technological discoveries: from fire to the latest in mobile telephony, computer technology and genetic engineering. It has been enriched by priceless contributions in painting, sculpture, architecture, music, literature, performing arts. Our civilization is also as precious as the lives of the individuals in it.

As uninvited guests to this party, the least we can do is not to spoil it with an act that rolls back this progress. It may take only one bomb to turn the Taj Mahal to rubbles, or to destroy a museum that houses some of the most treasured works of art. Or a brilliant scientist can create a monster that can destroy the Earth.

This is my suggestion for the second mission in our life: to contribute to the progress of the society, if we can; but in any case, not to cause damage to the many years of building the society to reach where it is today. A positive contribution would require skill, aptitude, commitment and opportunity; and not everyone may be able to leave an imprint on this

Earth. But avoiding acts that could damage the fabric of the society should be a conscious endeavor of every member of the society.

Once again, conscience assumes an important role. As we saw before, for all transgressions which are beyond the formal system of law and justice, there is religion and there is conscience. Religion has its moral codes (which are seldom updated with the times, because of the resistance from the orthodox followers of the religion), has a mass appeal; but would not be able to stand up to a rational scrutiny. Conscience also has moral codes, which are based on one's upbringing, the influences of parents, teachers and childhood friends, and are later modified, based on adult experiences. And conscience may not have the same degree of omniscience as is attributed to God, but it certainly knows all *your* deeds, and *your* thoughts. So instead of trying to please God, as the religion would want, why not just listen to your own conscience?

The Still Voice Within

I want to take the substitution of God and religion by conscience a step further by suggesting that our conscience can serve the psychological and emotional need that we have for God and religion, even when we agree that the concept of God is irrational.

It is not as if conscience has not been linked with God by the earlier generation of philosophers. Thomas Aquinas and Joseph Butler, both provide religious understanding of conscience, one as a moral tool of reason (Aquinas), the other an intuitive sense of God's voice (Butler); but whilst Aquinas and Butler argue for a God-given conscience, Sigmund

Freud's argument is based on the idea that the Conscience is manufactured from experiences and conditioning.

Conscience is a far more realistic version of a Personal God. It is designed to keep track of your deeds and thoughts, and it does not have to carry the burden of deeds and thoughts of other individuals – they have their own conscience to do it. Conscience also rewards and punishes you. It makes you feel happy, satisfied and confident in return for a good deed ('good' as defined by the moral code in your conscience), and guilty, ashamed and miserable as a punishment for a bad act. It cannot alter the conditions outside your control, while rewarding or punishing you. For example, before a job interview, it cannot 'miraculously' make the other worthy candidates disappear, or fumble during their interview. But it can infuse sufficient confidence in you that will reflect in your body language and how you present yourself at the interview. But this does not happen automatically – you need to build a rapport with your conscience, listen to 'the still voice within', and talk to it in your thoughts. A few moments of meditation can help. Say 'sorry' to it, when you sincerely regret your action, and are determined not to repeat it; say 'thank you' to it to strengthen your rapport and acknowledge the help it provided to you; and say 'please' when you want strength and inspiration, and if you sincerely believe that you deserve what you are asking for, and have worked for it. You cannot expect miracles.

As Swami Vivekanand has said:

> Talk to yourself once in a day, otherwise you may miss a meeting with an excellent person in this World.

In conclusion, I do not expect that religious people, who believe in God, pray to Him and are convinced that He will listen to their prayers, will alter their views on the basis of arguments I have provided. The theist belief may have very deep roots in their psyche. Nor do I believe that it is desirable for everybody in this world to discard their belief in God and religion. This could be detrimental to our civilization, unless those people are mature enough to follow the morals and ethics of our society, without the imaginary fear of someone watching them over their shoulders. But a strong belief in our own conscience can provide us with a more rational and realistic companion and confidant, whom we can depend on for guidance in whatever mission we have set for our life.